MY MOTHER'S SPICE CUPBOARD

Published by Hybrid Publishers

Melbourne Victoria Australia

© Elana Benjamin 2012

www.elanabenjamin.com

First published 2012

National Library of Australia Cataloguing-in-Publication entry:

Author: Benjamin, Elana.

Title: My mother's spice cupboard : a journey from Baghdad to
Bombay to Bondi / Elana Benjamin.

ISBN: 9781921665554 (pbk.)

Dewey number: 305.8924092

Subjects: Benjamin, Elana – Family.
Immigrants – New South Wales – Sydney – Biography.
Sephardim – India.
Sephardim – Iraq – Baghdad.
Jewish families – New South Wales – Sydney.

Cover design: Gittus Graphics ©

Printing and quality control in China by Tingelman Pty Ltd

My Mother's Spice Cupboard

*A journey from Baghdad
to Bombay to Bondi*

ELANA BENJAMIN

**HYBRID
PUBLISHERS**

For Mum and Dad,
and for Ariel,
without whom I would never have experienced the joys
of family and a Jewish home

And in memory of Melissa and Uncle Ike,
who always remain in my heart

CONTENTS

ACKNOWLEDGMENTS

Since beginning work on *My Mother's Spice Cupboard*, I have kept in mind the inspiring words of Theodor Herzl: 'If you will it, it is no dream.' I have been willing this book for a very long time, but without the involvement of the people below, *Spice Cupboard* would never have made the transition from dream to reality.

Thanks to Ian Bickerton at the University of New South Wales and Leanne Piggott at the University of Sydney for their encouragement of very early incarnations of *My Mother's Spice Cupboard*. I would never have had the courage to embark on such an ambitious project without their enthusiasm for some of the initial writing which evolved into parts of this book.

To Heather Ballantyne, for paving the way for me to work part-time so many years ago, so that I could spend a day a week researching and writing.

To all my relatives who spent countless hours sharing their memories, answering my questions and helping with fact checking: Hilda Jacob, Hannah Benjamin, Sarah Ezekiel, Florrie Marshall, Sammy Benjamin, Mozelle Breitstein, Fred Jacob, Gracie Lerno, Mike Benjamin, and especially my parents – Sheila and Abe Benjamin.

To my dear friends, Vivian van Gelder and Lisa Sarzin, for reviewing early drafts of the book and for being such staunch supporters over so many years. Also to Lisa for insisting that Hybrid Publishers was the right home for my manuscript. And to Leanne Berelowitz, for years of invaluable discussion about many of the themes which run through *Spice Cupboard*.

To Richard Beasley, for his sound publishing advice.

To my family: my brother Mike for his amazing memory and for being my ally in all things related to *Spice Cupboard*. To my parents and my mother-in-law Evie Gareb, who so willingly looked after my children so that I could work on the book.

And to my husband Ariel Winton, to whom I am deeply indebted for believing in me and supporting this project from the outset. Thank you for all you have done to make *My Mother's Spice Cupboard* materialise, and for being so willing to share your wisdom and expertise without ever being judgmental. Your love is the most precious of blessings, and I am so grateful to have you as my partner.

To Louis de Vries and Anna Rosner Blay at Hybrid Publishers, for taking on this project. Thank you for your dedication, advice, and kindness. It has been a privilege to work with you both.

And to my beloved grandparents – Hannah and Jacob Benjamin, Hilda and Eze Jacob – and my adored children, Zara and Asher Winton, without whom there would have been no story, and no impetus to record it.

PREFACE

My darlings Zara and Asher,

You have a rich and unusual heritage. *My Mother's Spice Cupboard* is the result of my desire to preserve at least part of this heritage and to record the story of our Sephardi Jewish family's emigration from Baghdad to Bombay (now Mumbai) to Sydney.

Unlike most other Australian Jews, my parents were born and grew up in Bombay, and my grandparents hailed from Iraq, Burma and India. My father's family immigrated to Sydney; my mother's to Los Angeles, both in the 1960s. My parents married in Sydney and raised their family here, alongside my father's many brothers and sisters and members of their former Bombay community. Despite being Jewish, my upbringing was greatly influenced by the food, language and culture of India and, to a lesser extent, Iraq.

I must admit that there have been times I have found being part of a large Sephardi family to be frustrating and even claustrophobic. Yet I sometimes envy the way my grandparents and parents lived in Bombay, and even how they lived when they moved to Sydney. Although they had little materially, they had a strong sense of family and of Baghdadi Jewish traditions, and their lives were essentially uncomplicated.

Growing up in Sydney as a first-generation Australian, in what felt like a community transplanted from Bombay into Bondi, was not so simple. The wider Jewish community was predominantly an Ashkenazi one. Many of them were unaware there had been a thriving Jewish community in India which had originated in Iraq. They were unfamiliar with the customs and traditions of the Baghdadi Jews, ate very different food from the spice-infused cooking I was used to, and peppered their English with Yiddish, rather than Arabic and Hindustani words and phrases.

My Mother's Spice Cupboard is predominantly the story of my father's family – the Benjamins – and to a lesser extent, my mother's family – the Jacobs – seen through my eyes. It is the story of what happened to a community which no longer exists, how its members built new lives for themselves in a different country and what it was like to grow up as one of their children. It is about how much things have changed over four generations in one family. Underlying the story is the importance of food and cooking to the Baghdadi Jews, which goes beyond the mere provision of sustenance to express warmth, love and hospitality.

Researching and writing this book has been a project which has spanned some ten years of my life. I started research even before I married and began transcribing audio tapes soon after. Putting it all together in a coherent format seemed like an insurmountable task. There were times I did not touch the manuscript for months, even a year. Other times – like in the months before you were born, Asher – I found myself writing crazily to meet self-imposed deadlines.

Much has transpired since I first had the idea of writing this book. Deaths, births, marriages, illness, plus the usual ups and downs of daily life. During all those events, *My Mother's Spice Cupboard* has been a constant which has kept me grounded. I feel incredibly privileged that some of the people I love most have shared so much of their personal history with me and so willingly given up their precious time to do so.

My beautiful children, this book is my gift to you. Although you are much too young to appreciate it now, I hope that one day you will treasure it.

All my love,
Mum
August 2011

Benjamin and Jacob Families

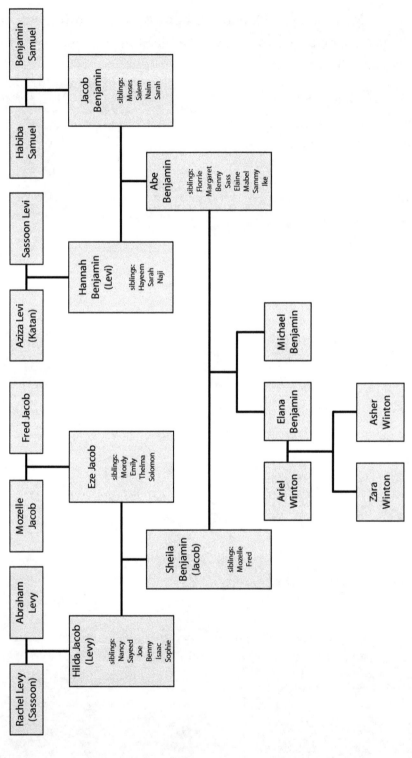

PART 1

BAGHDAD TO BOMBAY

1. NANA HANNAH

Hannah Benjamin, my paternal grandmother, was a strong-willed and determined woman. She was uncompromising and resilient. She had to be: in the space of less than twenty-five years she married, bore eleven babies, lost two of them and was widowed with nine children and no money. Not a recipe for an easy life.

Yet Nana Hannah had much to be proud of. At the time she died in October 2003, Hannah Benjamin had spawned a dynasty of nine children, nineteen grandchildren and twenty-eight great-grandchildren. The Benjamins are a warm, loving and community-minded family. All of Nana's children and grandchildren who have married have chosen Jewish spouses.

Despite being in awe of all Nana achieved in her lifetime, I would never wish to have lived her life. I doubt I would have survived! I distinctly remember one of my aunties' comments on the day of Nana's funeral: 'They don't make them like that anymore.' It's true. Nana was incredibly tough.

Nana and I are only two generations apart. Yet between Indian-Jewish grandmother and Australian-Jewish granddaughter is a huge chasm in values and attitudes. Nana faced many difficult situations during her lifetime and she had a remarkable lack of choice as to how she led her life. Rather than expending energy in frustration, she accepted her lot with a shrug of her shoulders and the utterance of three words: 'What to do?'

Nana grew up and raised her children within the confines of the small Baghdadi Jewish community of Bombay. It was simply expected that she would marry and have children. Once she had children, there was no question about which school she would send them to. The Jacob Sassoon Free High School, with its free tuition, Jewish education and hot lunches for the students, was the obvious choice. Nana didn't have the dilemma of work/life balance facing mothers today. She simply never worked outside the home and devoted her life to raising her children and looking after her family.

Nana was only forty-three years old when her husband died in 1956. Despite still being young, the thought of remarriage simply wasn't within her realm of possibility. When I asked her whether she ever considered marrying again, Nana unhesitatingly replied, 'No.' And then added emphatically, 'Not at all.'

I can't imagine being widowed today as a forty-three-year-old woman and not even *considering* the possibility of marrying another man. I can't fathom how Nana raised so many children even with a husband, let alone without him. I sometimes wish I could emulate Nana's ability to accept the status quo without questioning it, ruminating over it and resenting it. Sadly, I am not nearly as hardy as my grandmother.

I only came to know the details of Nana's early life when I was in my mid-twenties. The Nana of my childhood was physically close but emotionally distant. Although I saw her regularly, she wasn't a particularly influential figure in my life. It wasn't that we didn't get along. But by the time I was born, Nana was sixty-two years old. Certainly young by today's standards. By then, however, Nana had raised nine children of her own and had fourteen grandchildren before me. I was grandchild number fifteen and even more were to follow.

It wasn't just the sheer number of grandchildren that made it hard to get close to Nana. It was also her nature. Nana, although kind and loving, was not a particularly affectionate woman. The toughness that enabled her to get through the difficult times in her life translated into what I perceived – at least as child – to be a lack of warmth. I can barely recall any embrace we shared or time spent playing or simply chatting. Yet I saw Nana at least once a week during my entire childhood.

When I was growing up in the mid-1970s and '80s in the Sydney beachside suburb of Bondi, Nana lived only a ten-minute walk away from my family home. In fact, nearly all of my father's brothers and sisters and their families lived within a two-kilometre radius of our home. Every Saturday evening, all of Nana's children and all of her younger grandchildren – including me and my brother – would congregate at her apartment. I always looked forward to playing with my cousins, and my aunts and uncles were enticed by the promise of a Hannah Benjamin home-cooked Iraqi feast. These weekly family gatherings were filled with loud chatter, the sounds of children laughing and the aroma of spicy food.

We never ate dinner before going to Nana's house as she would always cook more than enough food for the twenty or so of us that would descend on her O'Brien Street home each week. Nana's apartment had two possible entries – a formal entry through the front door and another through the back door via the washing line and rubbish bins, which led straight to her kitchen. I don't remember anyone ever using the actual front door to get into Nana's apartment. We all entered straight through the kitchen, the smell of her cooking wafting through the concrete common area she shared with her neighbours.

Without fail, Nana fried up everyone's favourite snack – *aloomakalas* – each week. *Aloomakala* is a hybrid word: *aloo* means potato in Hindi and *makala* means fried in Arabic. Essentially they are potatoes which have been slowly deep-fried in oil and they are delicious. Nana's stove and oven were positioned directly in front of the kitchen door and many of us would pinch an *aloomakala* as soon as we were inside the kitchen. Often, they had just been removed from the boiling oil and were simply too hot to hold, so Nana would wrap them in paper towel. That didn't, however, stop me from burning my mouth as I impatiently took a bite before my *aloomakala* had cooled sufficiently.

Nobody makes *aloomakalas* these days (except maybe Aunty Florrie or Aunty Mabel on very special occasions) because they are loaded with oil and are not particularly healthy. But that wasn't a great concern to the Benjamins in the late 1970s and early '80s before they discovered a family predisposition to type 2 diabetes and high blood pressure.

Actually, none of Nana's food was the kind you would want to eat if you were watching your weight. I was never particularly interested in her other specialities: *coobas* (mince-meat balls covered in semolina and rice flour), beetroot *coobas* (the same with a beetroot sauce), *hamim* (also known as *hameen*: a dish of baked chicken in rice traditionally prepared for *Shabbat* [Saturday] lunch due to its very slow cooking time) and *chittarney* (a dry curry with lots of onion and vinegar). But Hannah's children and their spouses loved them and would devour her Iraqi and Indian cooking, regardless of the calories it contained.

Nana always had at least one packet of Lebanese pita bread put aside for our weekly visit. The pita was easily substituted for the more desirable but less available Indian roti and was supposed to be an accompaniment for Nana's food. *Junglee* that I was (Hindi for someone without manners, respect, or in my family, an appreciation of good food), I used to tear the bread and eat it in large strips on its own, filling my stomach with not very nutritious fried potato and white bread. The only other piece of Nana's cooking that I ate was her delicious sliced cucumber marinated in vinegar, which she prepared in an unglamorous but reliable old Moccona coffee jar.

Although I don't recall it, Nana must have been a coffee drinker because she had another old Moccona coffee jar positioned at child-friendly height on her buffet, filled with an assortment of lollies. There were Minties, sugar-coated spearmint leaves, fake candy bananas, chocolate freckles, milk bottles, and strawberries and creams. Yes, we loved going to Nana's each week!

Dinner was usually eaten with the TV – complete with massive spiral antenna on top – turned on in the background. The usual viewing schedule was *Young Talent Time*, *Mork and Mindy* and, in later years, *It's A Knockout*. The adults liked to play cards after dinner and 'Lucky 7' was a favourite. While they ate, the eight young cousins separated into two groups divided along gender lines: five girls and three boys. As far as I know, all the boys ever did was play cricket in the hallway, while the girls sang into the carpet sweeper (I don't think Nana even owned a vacuum cleaner).

On summer Saturday nights, all the cousins played cricket in the courtyard and tried to coax our parents into buying us ice-cream at the nearby Bondi Beach shops. We jumped up and down, pulled on the long washing line in Nana's courtyard and shouted, 'I scream, you scream, we all scream for ice-cream!' Our parents usually relented, if only to achieve some peace and quiet from eight screaming children.

Interestingly, aside from cooking, I'm not sure what Nana did during this time when her family descended on her home. I don't remember interacting much with her, other than being told off for causing chaos in her perfectly tidy house. '*Buss*! So much mess y'all made?' she would shout at us in her uniquely Indian-English constructed sentence. What she meant was: 'Enough! What a mess all of you have made.' Having raised nine children of her own, she knew how to keep her grandchildren in line. We were never scared of her in the way that her own children had been (my father recalls being terrified of her when he was growing up), but I don't think any of us had a close bond with her either.

Nana certainly seemed happy to have the company of her

family and to have her home filled once more with laughter and chatter, but it seemed to me that she was relieved when we finally left each Saturday night and she could return her apartment to its usual state of peace and order.

Nana was really quite a character. She was well connected within the Sydney Baghdadi Jewish community and was always up to speed with the latest *hadoosh* (Arabic for 'gossip'). She had copies of the latest *TV Week* and *New Idea* magazines stacked under her coffee table and knew all the celebrity news. She had a phenomenal memory and was always aware of what each of her children and grandchildren were doing from week to week.

Nana was obviously proud of her family, and photographs of her children and grandchildren hung all around her apartment. The wedding photos of my parents and my aunts and uncles were displayed on the walls above her couch, and on the buffet were photos of each one of her grandchildren: baby photos, school photos, graduation photos.

I always loved to look at Nana's collection of photos when I visited her. One of my favourites was a black-and-white shot of Nana dancing with Uncle Benny at Uncle Sass' wedding in 1969. Nana was so young that I could hardly recognise her.

At the time, it never seemed strange to me that among all these photos, Nana didn't have even one of her late husband. It was only in hindsight that I noticed that she never talked about the man she had married and she didn't wear a wedding ring (I later discovered that it had become so worn out that she stopped wearing it.)

The first time I ever saw Nana's wedding photo was in the same year that I got married, when I was already twenty-six years old. I think that may have been the first photo I had ever seen of my grandfather, Jacob Benjamin.

2. BAGHDADI BEGINNINGS

Jacob Benjamin died long before I was born. In fact, he did not live long enough to see any of his grandchildren. So although I sometimes refer to him as 'Papa' Jacob, I use the term 'Papa' out of respect; in my mind he is simply 'Jacob'. Although he was my father's father, he was a man I never knew and a man who was rarely spoken of while I was growing up.

The little I was told about my paternal grandfather included that he was a well-liked and well-respected member of Bombay's Baghdadi Jewish community. And that of his five sons, it is my father who is most like him in temperament and mannerisms: softly spoken, kind, calm and gentle.

When I started seeking more detailed knowledge about Jacob Benjamin, I noticed that no one had anything negative to say about him. Of course, he couldn't have been flawless. But I think the fact of his untimely death left him somewhat suspended in time; Jacob was only fifty-four years old when he died and most of his children hadn't yet reach adulthood. Even when he was alive, Jacob's children didn't get to spend much time with him as he was so busy working. Nevertheless, they all adored him and even today, Jacob's children affectionately refer to their father as 'Daddy'.

None of Jacob Benjamin's nine children had the benefit of watching their father grow old; they didn't have him by their side when they left India and emigrated to Australia. And so it seems that my father and his siblings, even though they now have children and grandchildren of their own, still hold on to that childlike quality of believing their father was infallible. If only Jacob Benjamin had lived longer, they could have gained more insight into his strengths and weaknesses, and received his guidance on so many aspects of their own lives.

Jacob Benjamin was the eldest of five children and was born in Baghdad, Iraq, in December 1902. At the time, there was a substantial Jewish population in Baghdad.

Iraq came under British rule during World War I, and during the war, Jacob's father was conscripted into the British army. He was never heard from again, presumed killed at war. Having lost her husband, Jacob's mother Habiba feared for her eldest son's life; Jacob was at an age where he too could soon be conscripted into the British army.

So Habiba insisted that Jacob flee Baghdad for Bombay to escape army duties. It was 1917 when Habiba disguised Jacob, merely fifteen years old at the time, by dressing him as an Arab and sending him to Bombay with his uncles (Habiba's half-brothers). Ironically, Jacob's two uncles were younger than Jacob himself, so Jacob was responsible for looking after them!

The three young men travelled on donkeys through bandit-infested forests in order to catch a boat from the Iraqi port city of Basra to Bombay. Once in Bombay, the three men lived with Jacob's grandfather, *Chacham* Avraham Tahan (whom everyone knew as *Chacham* Avraham; *chacham* being the Hebrew word for wise man or scholar) and his wife.

Fifteen-year-old Jacob began working as a tram driver in Bombay in order to earn a living. His mother Habiba and his four siblings eventually followed Jacob to Bombay, but not until after the end of the war in 1918.

Jacob Benjamin with his mother and siblings weren't the first Iraqi Jews to leave Baghdad for Bombay. Almost a century earlier, in the 1820s and '30s, considerable numbers of Iraqi Jews had left

Iraq for India in order to avoid persecution. Indeed, by the time Jacob arrived in India, a well-established Iraqi Jewish community not only existed, but was prospering in Bombay.

When Jacob Benjamin arrived in Bombay in 1917, a five-year-old girl named Hannah Levi was also living there. Hannah's family were members of Bombay's Baghdadi Jewish community and her parents had also made the journey from Iraq to India. Years later, Hannah would become Jacob's bride.

Hannah Levi's Family

Hannah's parents, Sassoon and Aziza Levi, were married in Baghdad, Iraq. Astonishingly, at the time they married, Aziza was only fourteen years old. Equally as remarkable, Aziza's husband Sassoon was almost twice her age and already had three children from his first wife, who had since died.

Sassoon and Aziza's marriage was an arranged one and I'm certain that Aziza didn't have any power to veto the choice of her husband-to-be. Although it was common practice at the time for Iraqi Jewish girls to be married off at such a young age, it is still shocking to me that my great-grandmother became a wife and stepmother when she was only a child herself.

Aziza must have been an extraordinary woman. I am told that she raised her three stepchildren as if they were her own, which must have been extremely challenging. This is especially so given Aziza and Sassoon's difficulties with their biological children: the couple had a staggering sixteen children together, but only four of them survived to reach adulthood. Aziza and Sassoon's babies – including two sets of twins – kept dying, one after another, until eventually Aziza, heartbroken, convinced her husband to move from Iraq to India in the hope that a new country would give them a fresh start. The fact that a Baghdadi Jewish community existed in Bombay undoubtedly influenced their decision to relocate there.

In Bombay, Aziza gave birth to a son and named him Hayeem,

derived from the Hebrew word for 'life'. He was their first surviving child and was followed by fraternal twin girls – Hannah and Sarah, and another son, Naji. Aziza then had another daughter, but she too died when she was only a year old.

Hannah Levi – better known to me as Nana Hannah – and her twin sister Sarah were born in Poona (now Pune), India, approximately 160 kilometres south of Bombay. Nana always maintained that her date of birth was 16 July 1912. However, Nana's birth date has been a source of debate and amusement within the Benjamin family.

The Nana Hannah/Aunty Sarah birthday controversy is this: Nana and Aunty Sarah were twins who paradoxically claimed – at least as adults – to have different birthdays. Nana celebrated her birthday every year on July 16. Yet Aunty Sarah insisted that she was born almost one year later, in May 1913. The two sisters even had different birthdates on their passports. Both as stubborn as each other, each sister was adamant that she was correct.

Of course, all Nana's very loyal children (who also know Nana's impeccable recollection of important dates) were convinced that Nana was correct and that Aunty Sarah simply didn't want to admit she was actually a year older than she claimed. Neither sister ever had a birth certificate to prove who was correct, and without official records, their birthday dispute raged for years.

I visited Aunty Sarah in London in 2001 and finally solved the mystery. Aunty Sarah admitted to me that when she emigrated to London from Bombay, she enrolled in an educational course and nominated a birth date of May 1913 so she could get into the course. Aunty Sarah has since conceded that Nana was correct regarding their date of birth.

Soon after Hannah and Sarah were born in July 1912, Sassoon and Aziza moved their family from Poona to the Bombay suburb of

Byculla. Sassoon and Aziza were observant Jews; they kept a kosher home (observed the Jewish dietary laws) and, without a kosher butcher shop in Bombay at the time, Aziza koshered her own meat which had been slaughtered according to Jewish law. Sassoon was a skilled *mohel* (a man qualified to circumcise Jewish baby boys) and he taught his children, including his twin daughters, to read Hebrew. Both Sassoon and Aziza regularly studied Torah, the five Books of Moses.

Despite their religious convictions, Aziza and Sassoon sent Hannah and Sarah to the Clare Road Convent School, a Catholic school in Bombay, due to its high standard of education. But the twins transferred to Bombay's only Jewish school in the Fourth Standard (equivalent to 7th Grade): the Jacob Sassoon Free School.

Hannah didn't like either the Catholic or the Jewish school much. Aged twelve, a resolute young Hannah decided that she no longer wanted to go to school. I have already described her as a very strong-minded and determined woman. Even at this young age Hannah knew exactly what she wanted. And it was that she didn't want to attend school. She preferred to stay home and help her mother cook. Hannah pleaded with her parents not to force her to go to school and eventually they agreed.

At home with her mother Aziza, Hannah learned to cook traditional Iraqi Jewish food. She became an exceptional cook and drew on her cooking skills constantly when she had a large family of her own, and in her later life when her children had left home.

As a teenager, Hannah received a number of marriage proposals. In the late 1920s in Bombay's Baghdadi Jewish community, most marriages were arranged by matchmakers. So in fact it was Hannah's mother Aziza who received the proposals and it was Aziza who decided who her daughter would marry. Had he been alive, Hannah's father would have received the marriage proposals, but Sassoon had died in 1928 when Hannah was only sixteen years old.

Aziza rejected all the early proposals because she considered Hannah too young to marry. Remembering Aziza had been only fourteen years old when she married, it speaks volumes that Aziza didn't want her daughter to become a child bride like she had been.

But in 1929, Aziza accepted a proposal for seventeen-year-old Hannah to marry a twenty-seven-year-old man named Jacob Benjamin – the same Jacob Benjamin who had been living in Bombay for over ten years, having fled Baghdad dressed as an Arab. Papa Jacob.

3. HANNAH AND JACOB'S WEDDING

Jewish weddings in the Benjamin family are always big celebrations, filled with plenty of singing and dancing, and enormous amounts of food. And there's always entertainment provided by the more gregarious relatives who dance with glasses of alcohol or soft drink precariously balanced on their heads. Yes, the Benjamins love a good wedding party. And Hannah and Jacob's wedding was certainly a huge celebration for both the Levi and Benjamin families.

Once the match between Hannah and Jacob had been made and then approved by Aziza, Hannah had no choice but to marry Jacob. Aziza did not ask, but told her daughter Hannah that she would be marrying Jacob Benjamin. Like her mother a generation earlier, Hannah had no say in the process of a husband being chosen for her.

Luckily for Hannah, her first impressions of her husband-to-be were good ones. She had seen Jacob at a party – a *brit milah* (circumcision of a Jewish baby boy) – and liked him. Jacob, she told me, was a handsome young man, with dark hair and brown eyes. The photos I have seen of him attest to this.

I asked Nana whether she liked Jacob's immediate and extended family. She replied, 'Yes, I respected them.' Interestingly, this response didn't directly answer my question, but it showed that for Nana, it was respect rather than feelings of 'like' or 'dislike' which were important.

Nana's response was also indicative of the change which has occurred within two generations: for Nana, respect was a fundamental element in family relationships. Over time, however, the value of respect has declined in importance and has been replaced with concepts of 'like', 'admire' and 'love'. The mantra of 'respecting your elders' is no longer blindly followed. Respect must now be earned.

Aziza Levi gave Jacob Benjamin's family a dowry of 1,500 rupees in support of Hannah and Jacob's impending marriage. This was a sizeable amount of money at the time – the equivalent of one year's salary.

Hannah and Jacob had a big engagement party at Hannah's aunt's house. The party consisted of a dinner on a Saturday night after *Shabbat* (the Jewish day of rest). Chickens were slaughtered and then cooked, and there were four Arab belly dancers. Hannah and Jacob's mothers, Aziza and Habiba respectively, arranged the engagement party. This was Aziza's first daughter to marry so the engagement party was an important occasion for her.

Prior to their wedding, Hannah and Jacob never went out alone in Bombay. While they were engaged, Jacob did go and visit his bride-to-be each week and would bring a small present for her each time. But Hannah was so shy that if she was walking on the street and saw her future husband, she would cross the street to avoid having to talk to him!

Hannah Levi married Jacob Benjamin on a Sunday afternoon on 6 April 1930 at the Keneseth Eliyahoo Fort Synagogue in Bombay, India. Neither Hannah nor Jacob's father was alive to see his children marry. Hannah's step-brother Salah (from her father Sassoon's first marriage) walked her down the aisle.

Eighteen-year-old Hannah was ten years younger than her *chatan*, her groom. The wedding was not a particularly extravagant affair. Hannah did have a new dress made by an Indian tailor for her wedding day. It was a three-quarter length white dress. Typical of the Baghdadi Jews of Bombay, her dress wasn't a sari-type traditional Indian gown but was more British looking, with short sleeves and a round neckline. India was under British rule at the time and the Baghdadi Jews tended to align themselves with the British.

Hannah also wore a veil that was given to her by a friend and had a simple wreath of flowers in her hair. Jacob gave Hannah a gold wedding ring and Hannah's mother gave Jacob's family gifts of silver and copper coins. The wedding was paid for by Hannah's family.

When I look at Hannah and Jacob's wedding photograph today, I notice that both the bride and groom look incredibly solemn. Jacob's dark hair is perfectly combed back. He is wearing Gandhi style round-framed glasses and is holding a pair of white gloves. He has a small moustache and stands upright. Unsmiling, he looks the perfect British gentleman. I can't see him wearing a *kippah* (skullcap) but I know he and Hannah had a traditional Jewish wedding under a *chuppah* (Jewish marriage canopy).

In the same photograph, Hannah is sitting down and holding a bunch of flowers which cascade from her lap onto the floor. Her hair is short and looks quite stylish. She certainly looks older than her eighteen years. Only their Indian-looking bridesmaids – Hannah's sister Sarah and Jacob's sister, also Sarah – give any clue as to the country in which they married.

After the *chuppah* at the Synagogue, a dinner was held at Hannah's mother's home for the bride and groom's respective families. Cooks, rather than any family members, prepared the kosher dinner.

Hannah told me that she didn't think she was too young to marry, and indeed, she was happy to get married. Despite their marriage being arranged, Hannah grew to love Jacob as she got to know him. She described her husband as kind, gentle and quiet, and said that he wasn't difficult to live with.

It is amazing to think that this couple – a couple who barely knew each other before they married in Bombay – spawned a dynasty of Benjamins. Yet not one of Hannah and Jacob's many descendants lives in India today.

Wedding photo of Hannah and Jacob Benjamin, Bombay, 1930

Adults (left to right): Hannah's sister Sarah, Jacob Benjamin, Hannah Benjamin, Jacob's brother Moses, Jacob's sister Sarah
Flower girls in front row are Iris Moses (Jacob's aunt!) and Sarah Ellis (Hannah's cousin)

4. SOME HISTORY

The word 'Sephardi' originates from the Hebrew word for Spain, *Sfarad*. But not all Sephardi Jews are of Spanish origin. Many Sephardi Jews – like the Benjamins – have their roots in Baghdad, Iraq. I can't trace my ancestors much past my great-great-grandparents, but it seems likely they were in Baghdad for some time.

Baghdad is close to the site of ancient Babylon, where the Jews were exiled in the year 6 BCE.[1] It's not clear whether there has been a continuous Jewish presence in Baghdad since that time, but it is well accepted that Baghdad was a flourishing centre of Jewish life during the Middle Ages. At that time, Jewish religious authorities (*geonim*) were located in Baghdad and as a result Baghdad set religious standards for the Jewish world.

Historians disagree as to whether any Jews remained in Baghdad between the end of the 14th century and the early years of the 16th century, but agree that there was an influx of Jews to Baghdad in the 16th century. From that time, there was a substantial Jewish community in Iraq until the early 1950s.

In 1948, there were some 135,000 Jews living in Iraq,[2] which is more than the entire Jewish population of Australia today. 1948 was also the year in which the State of Israel was established. Iraqi Jews had periodically experienced persecution in the decades preceding Israel's establishment. In particular, there was a violent pogrom against the Jews of Baghdad in June 1941, which the Jews referred to as the *farhud*. Estimates vary, but around 200 Jews were killed and hundreds more were injured in two days of riots.[3]

The years prior to the establishment of Israel saw frequent demonstrations in Iraq against the Jews and against Zionism. When war broke out following the end of the British Mandate of Palestine, hundreds of Jews in Iraq were rounded up and thrown into jail without trial, accused of passing military secrets to Zionists in Palestine.[4] Iraqi Jews also began to experience economic discrimination and other restrictions. For example, they were prohibited from moving from one location to another in Iraq and there were restrictions preventing their attendance at schools and hospitals.[5] Between July 1948 and December 1949, around 800 Jews were dismissed from the public service, without notice, severance pay or pensions.[6]

Iraqi Jews began to realise there was no future for them in the country which had been their home for so many years. In 1950, the Iraqi Government passed legislation allowing Jews to leave Iraq for good, provided they renounced their citizenship. Initially, Jews were slow to take up the offer to leave. Eventually, however, between 1950 and 1952 some 120,000–130,000 Iraqi Jews were airlifted to Israel via Operation Ezra and Nechamia. When Israel's rescue of the Jews of Iraq was complete, only 6,000 Jews remained in Iraq. In 2008, there were fewer than ten Jews in all of Iraq.[7]

It was therefore a blessing that Jacob Benjamin fled Iraq in 1917, decades before the *farhud* and subsequent persecution of Jews in Iraq. By the 1950s, Baghdad was but a distant memory to Jacob, who by that time had a large family integrated into the Baghdadi Jewish community of Bombay.

From Iraq to India: The Baghdadi Jews

The term 'Baghdadi Jew' has come to encompass not only Jews from Iraq, but also Jews from Syria, Aden and Yemen (all of whom spoke Arabic) and even Jews from Persia and Afghanistan (who did not speak Arabic).[8] The first Baghdadi Jews began arriving in India in the 18th century.

David Sassoon (1792–1864) is probably the most famous Baghdadi Jew to have settled in Bombay after leaving Baghdad. David was born at a time when the safety of his family and the whole Jewish community of Baghdad was in danger. As David fled Baghdad for India, so did many other Jews, seeking the religious freedom and trading benefits which were reportedly available in British-ruled India.[9] In Bombay, David entered the import-export business and established the firm of David Sassoon and Company. The demand for India's cotton placed the Sassoon family into unprecedented prosperity and influence.[10]

Aside from being a successful businessman, David Sassoon was an Orthodox Jew and exceptional philanthropist. Word spread among the poor Jews in Baghdad and throughout the Ottoman Empire that employment was available in Bombay with David Sassoon's firm. Remarkably, he arranged food, housing and medical care for the new arrivals and even established the David Sassoon Benevolent Institution (now a public library called the David Sassoon Library, built in 1847) to provide education for their children. The children were also taught ritual slaughtering of animals so that they could eat kosher meat if their jobs took them to places without established Jewish communities. In 1861, David built the Magen David Synagogue in the Bombay suburb of Byculla, the best location in Bombay at the time. The Synagogue Compound contained a hostel for travellers, a *mikvah* (ritual bath) and a *Talmud Torah* (religious school).[11]

David Sassoon's philanthropy in the Jewish community and in India as a whole was carried on by subsequent generations of Sassoons.

David's son Elias Sassoon established his own, separate firm: E. D. Sassoon and Company. When Elias died, his son Jacob took over the business. In the 1880s, Jacob Sassoon actively recruited workers from Baghdad, and at one point the textile mills of his company employed 15,000 people, although only a small number of these were Jews.[12] The firm's policy was to give preference to Jews in initial employment, but not necessarily in promotion.[13] The promise of jobs in the Sassoon Mills encouraged Jews from Baghdad to uproot their families and move to Bombay.

In 1884, Jacob Sassoon built the Keneseth Eliyahoo Synagogue in the Fort area of Bombay. He also endowed cemeteries; funds for feeding poor, elderly and disabled Jews; and a free high school for Baghdadi children.

The economic empire built by the Sassoons, together with their charitable activities, led them to become known as the 'Rothschilds of the East'. By the beginning of the 20th century, Baghdadi Jews arriving in Bombay to start new lives had synagogues in which to pray, a free Jewish school in which to educate their children and a source of employment in the Sassoons Mills. It is unsurprising then that Baghdadi Jews, facing persecution in their countries of birth, chose Bombay as their new home. Allowed to practise their religion freely and supported by institutions established by the Sassoons, their small community flourished.

Hannah and Jacob Benjamin and their children used many of the structures the Sassoons put in place in Bombay. They married at the Keneseth Eliyahoo Synagogue and prayed at the Magen David Synagogue. Jacob worked at the Sassoon Mills and all of Hannah and Jacob's children attended the Jacob Sassoon School.

Even when they were at their most numerous in 1951, there were only 5000 Jews in all of India – and that small figure encompasses not only those Baghdadi Jews living in Bombay, but those in all of India.[14] It was estimated that before the end of the 20th century, barely 200 Baghdadi Jews remained in all of India.[15] Today, there are barely any Baghdadi Jews in Bombay or in any other part of India.

5. BOMBAY'S JEWS

Hannah and Jacob Benjamin married and raised their family when the Baghdadi Jewish community of Bombay was at its prime. During the 1930s, '40s and early '50s the community flourished, although it was neither large nor wealthy. It followed the traditions of the Ben Ish Hai (the late *Chacham* Yosef Hayim of Baghdad) and the synagogues followed the Baghdadi mode of prayer.

The families which made up the community tended to live in the Bombay suburbs of Byculla and Colaba, primarily because the Sassoon-built synagogues were in those two areas. The poorer families lived in Byculla; the wealthier in Colaba. Despite the proximity of Byculla to Colaba – it is only nine kilometres between them – there was a sharp divide between the inhabitants of each area.

The historian Joan Roland notes that those who lived in Byculla were considered unrefined and were looked down on by the wealthier Baghdadis who lived in the Fort and Colaba districts.[16] Byculla Jews sent their children to the Sir Jacob Sassoon Free School, whereas Fort Jews went to private Christian schools which had higher standards.[17] Even in Habonim (Zionist youth group) camps the two groups remained apart.[18] Byculla Jews were considered very clannish; they joined Byculla groups, went to synagogue and school with Byculla friends and had no contact with the outside world until they grew up and got jobs.[19] Fort Jews preferred not to 'intermarry' with them.[20]

Although Hannah and Jacob Benjamin married in the Fort Synagogue of Bombay, they never lived in the wealthier Colaba district of Bombay. Rather, their home was in Byculla.

Joan Roland's account of the Byculla Jews (in *Jews in British India: Identity in a Colonial Era*) is certainly accurate in relation to the experiences of the Benjamins. The Byculla community was a very insular one. The Benjamins, together with other Jewish families, lived sheltered lives in an almost self-imposed ghetto. Almost all of the Jews lived in the same few streets, many in the same apartment blocks, and the community's key institutions (the Magen David Synagogue and the Jacob Sassoon School) were only a few minutes walk away from their homes.

The Synagogue and School

The Magen David Synagogue was built in Byculla in 1861 by David Sassoon. It wasn't large enough to accommodate the increasing Jewish congregation and so in 1910 it was enlarged and renovated by Sir Jacob Sassoon, David Sassoon's grandson. The Magen David Synagogue was the spiritual and physical focus of Jewish life in Byculla; it was the heart of the small community.

The elementary school, also built by David Sassoon, was later expanded into a high school by his grandson Jacob Sassoon and renamed The Sir Jacob Sassoon Free High School. The school was founded in 1903, almost forty years after the Synagogue. It was, however, located in the same grounds as the Synagogue. The combined area was known as 'the Synagogue Compound' and the community's adults and children used the large grounds as a place to meet each other and socialise.

The plaque outside the entrance to the School reads:

Jacob Sassoon Free School

This institution was presented to the Jewish community and endowed with a liberal donation of Rs: 110,000 on the 17th day of April 1903, by the generous benevolence of Mr Jacob Elias Sassoon for the free education of Jewish

boys and girls in Hebrew and English, which amount
he subsequently supplemented by a further sum of Rs:
40,000 making a total endowment fund of Rs: 150,000,
investing and handing over same to a Board of Trustees
for the control thereof.

This donation of 150,000 rupees was an enormous amount
of money. Bearing in mind that Nana Hannah's dowry of 1,500
rupees was the equivalent of one year's salary in around 1930,
Jacob Sassoon donated one hundred times this amount for the free
education of Jewish children.

The Jacob Sassoon Free School was an English medium school
that taught up to matriculation standard (university/college
entrance) and was always considered a Baghdadi school. In the
early years, the school was seen as a charitable institution for poor
and destitute Jews, and students who passed the matriculation
were offered employment in the textile mills of E. D. Sassoon and
in other local firms.

After 1925, however, with the appointment of a new
headmistress, the school flourished. Between 1926 and 1930,
attendance rose from 246 to 410.[21] Children from more affluent
families began to attend, examination results improved and the
educational inspection reports were good. By the 1930s the school
had to refuse admission to children because of lack of room; there
were around 200 children on the waiting list.[22]

However, the school declined in the 1940s and '50s and
discipline became slack.[23] Many wealthy children returned to
the private Christian-run schools and only poorer Baghdadis
remained, partly because they depended on the free meals and
medical check-ups which were also provided.

Nevertheless, at the time Hannah and Jacob Benjamin lived in
Bombay, the Jacob Sassoon School was a fundamental institution of
the Baghdadi Jewish community and ensured that Jewish children

were able to receive a free Jewish education. Parents who sent their children to the school did give a monthly donation towards fees, but it was really only a token donation; it was given according to the parents' means and so some parents gave nothing at all.

School students were also provided with a strictly kosher hot lunch every day, which was paid for by the Sassoon Trust. The school contained a large lunch room and lunchtime was staggered to prevent overcrowding. Nana Hannah, who attended the school for a few years, remembered being served 'doll (*dhal*) and rice' for lunch every Friday.

It is difficult to imagine such an institution existing in any Jewish community today – a school where not only was education free, hot lunch and medical check-ups provided, but where students who may have already eaten breakfast in their own homes received a soft-boiled egg and mug of milk each morning.

The Byculla Jews, poor as most of them were, were very fortunate to be able to give their children a Jewish education. The Jacob Sassoon School enabled the Baghdadi Jews to formally pass down their customs and traditions to their children.

Moreover, the Baghdadi Jews of Bombay were able to live freely as Jews and have complete religious freedom at the same time as their Jewish brethren were being murdered in Nazi-occupied Europe. The Byculla community's focus on Judaism, family and community allowed the Baghdadi Jews to live a Jewish life in a way that many Jews throughout history could only have dreamt of.

6. THE BENJAMINS OF BYCULLA

When Hannah and Jacob were first married, they lived in an apartment on Vasover Street within the Byculla neighbourhood of Nagpada. It wasn't unusual for extended families to live together, and Hannah and Jacob shared the Vasover Street apartment with Jacob's mother Habiba and Jacob's brother and sister-in-law. Later, they all moved; Hannah and Jacob to an apartment in the Synagogue Compound and then to Peerkhan Street; and Habiba across the road from them.

Newly-married Hannah and Jacob soon started a family, although Hannah's first pregnancy ended in miscarriage in April 1931. Nana told me that it then took her 'a long time' to get pregnant again. It probably seemed like an eternity at the time, but it was actually less than a year later when Hannah fell pregnant in January 1932. Hannah and Jacob's first child was a girl, Florence (Florrie), born only three months after Hannah's twentieth birthday.

After that time, Hannah seemed to have no trouble falling pregnant and she was pregnant another ten times over a period of twenty-one years. Sadly, one baby girl born to Hannah and Jacob died at only ten days old and another of Hannah's pregnancies delivered a stillborn boy at full term. The other pregnancies, however, delivered healthy children.

I asked Nana Hannah if she had always thought she was going to have so many children. She answered with a resounding 'no!' and then told me a story from her days as a young married woman. At the time, Hannah was married but childless; a state that wouldn't last for long. She was on a bus in Bombay and a woman who was a complete stranger came up to Hannah and said: 'You're fat, you won't get any children.' (This phrase of 'getting' children, which means 'having children' is another peculiarity of the English-Hindustani vernacular spoken by the Baghdadi Jews of Bombay.)

The woman's prediction was completely unfounded, yet the story stuck in Hannah's mind some seventy years later! As if trying to prove this stranger wrong, Hannah and Jacob produced nine children: five boys and four girls. Florrie in 1932, Margaret in 1934, Benjamin (Benny) in 1935, Sassoon (Sass) in 1938, Elaine in 1940, Abraham (Abe) – my father – in 1943, Mabel in 1945, Samuel (Sammy) in 1947 and Isaac (Ike) in 1953. Being a twin herself, Hannah thought she might have twins, but among all her descendants there is only one set of twins.

My father Abe, Hannah and Jacob's sixth child, was named after Jacob's grandfather, *Chacham* Avraham. And Abe, like his brothers, was given his father's name – Jacob – as his middle name; it was common practice in India to nominate the father's name as a child's middle name. Society was so patriarchal that even wives and daughters took on their husbands' and fathers' first name as their middle name (and so, much to my amusement, all Nana's aluminium *patilas* [pots] had the initials 'HJB' engraved into them: Hannah Jacob Benjamin).

By the time my father Abe was born in December 1943, Hannah and Jacob had moved to a three-room apartment on Nagpada Road, also in Byculla. The apartment block in which they lived was named 'Dil-Aram-Manzil', which is Hindi for the 'peaceful heart building'. I am not sure how peaceful it was for such a large family to live in such a small home – the whole apartment contained three rooms, plus a kitchen and washroom, maybe 75 square metres in total – but I do know they had many happy times there.

Of the seven apartments in the Dil-Aram-Manzil building in which the Benjamins lived, four were rented by Baghdadi Jewish families. As Joan Roland described, the Baghdadi Jews tended to stick together and didn't mix much with non-Jews, nor with the Bene Israel or Cochini Jews who lived in India at the same time. Nevertheless, there was no anti-Semitism and all three strands of Indian Jews lived in harmony with their non-Jewish neighbours.

My father and his brothers and sisters grew up playing on the streets of Nagpada and in the Synagogue Compound with each other and with the children of their Baghdadi Jewish neighbours. Their lives were incredibly rich with the company of their immediate and extended families, and the support of their fellow community members. The doors of the Benjamins' small apartment and of the apartments of their neighbours were left open all day, and family and friends dropped in and out of each other's homes at any time, chatting and sharing food they had cooked.

Some afternoons, Hannah, her mother-in-law Habiba and some of the neighbours set up the *hookah* (also known as the 'hubble bubble') and had a smoke. The *hookah* was a large pipe which utilised water and indirect heat for smoking. The tobacco mixture usually comprised tobacco mixed with rose petals and it sat in a clay pot on top of a large bowl of water. A thick pipe was connected to the water bowl and when the water steamed up the women inhaled the tobacco smoke.

As they smoked, the women no doubt gossiped and exchanged recipes and child-rearing advice. I wonder if my grandmother, my great-grandmother and their neighbours appreciated the relaxed and unhurried pace of their lives, or if they ever yearned for more. My guess is that most of them didn't give such indulgent thoughts even a moment's reflection.

Both Hannah and Jacob's mothers, Aziza and Habiba respectively, played important parts in the Benjamins' lives. Jacob's mother Habiba lived across the road from Dil-Aram-Manzil, with Jacob's two brothers Salem and Naim. Hannah's mother Aziza also lived within walking distance of the Benjamins' small apartment, first with her children Sarah and Naji, and then only with Naji after Sarah married.

Although the Benjamin children grew up without grandfathers, they were close to both their grandmothers, whom they affectionately referred to as Nani Aziza and Nani Habiba (*nani* is the Hindi word for 'grandmother'). Habiba lived to see all nine of Hannah and Jacob's children, and Aziza saw all except for their youngest child, Isaac.

I must admit that I somewhat envy the richness of the family and communal life enjoyed by the Benjamins. Yet their daily existence was by no means idyllic; they lacked material comforts which are now taken for granted, at least in the West. Living in Dil-Aram-Manzil on Nagpada Road, the Benjamins had no running water, no refrigeration, no toilet in their apartment, cramped living conditions and few possessions. In spite of these living conditions, the Benjamins paradoxically enjoyed the help of two *aaya*s (maids). These aayas performed much of the mundane work inherent in a home without modern labour-saving devices and with so many mouths to feed.

It was Hannah, however, who ran her home. She was incredibly strict with her children, all of whom remember being terrified of her. Nana acknowledged to me that it was she, not Jacob, who disciplined their nine children: 'I used to be the boss in the house,' she admitted. 'The children used to fear me more than their father.' Of Hannah, my father Abe says, 'We knew that her word was law and there was no room for negotiation.'

The way that Hannah, Jacob and their children lived their lives in Bombay was, both literally and metaphorically, worlds away from the way I grew up in Sydney in the 1970s and 1980s.

Benjamin family photo, Bombay, 1947
Back row (left to right): Florrie, Benny, Margaret
Front row: Elaine, Mabel, Hannah (pregnant with Sammy), Jacob,
Habiba, Abe, Sass

7. LIVING ON NAGPADA ROAD

The Benjamins' apartment on Nagpada Road can only be described, at least by Western standards today, as completely overcrowded. Their apartment consisted of only three rooms, yet it housed twelve people (eleven plus the aaya).

There was a dining room and one large room with a fixed timber partition which divided that space into two smaller rooms: a bedroom and a living room. Each night, the living room was converted into a second bedroom in order to provide enough space for all the family members to sleep. In that makeshift second bedroom, either a foldaway lounge was opened or spare mattresses were laid on the floor. In total, about three or four mattresses were placed on the floor and the rest of the family slept on beds.

The main bedroom had three beds and each bed was shared by two children, even though the beds were only slightly wider than a single bed. My father Abe shared a bed with his younger brother Sammy and assures me that it wasn't too cramped. Hannah and Jacob didn't sleep in a separate room to their children.

There could have been little privacy in such a set-up, but none of the family members seemed to mind their nightly slumber party. Still, I can't help but compare it to the way we live in the West today, where even if the few children in a home don't have their own bedrooms, they certainly don't share them with their parents.

In addition to the three rooms, the Benjamins' apartment also contained a kitchen and a bathroom. Contrary to its name, the bathroom didn't actually contain a bath. It didn't contain a toilet either.

Instead, common toilets were situated outside the apartment: two toilets for each floor of the building. Like all Indian toilets, there was no Western-style cistern and raised seat, only a hole in the ground.

When the youngest of the Benjamin children, Isaac, was born, all of his siblings were still living at home. My father estimates that at one time, there must have been twenty-two to twenty-five people (from three separate tenancies on the same floor of the building) sharing only two toilets.

The so-called 'bathroom' was approximately four square metres, all tiled. Without a toilet or bath, it was really more of a washroom, a washroom without running water.

Instead of running water, the apartment had water lines which the municipality of Bombay pumped into residents' homes at specific hours every morning and evening. From this mains supply, it was up to each household to fill up drums and other containers with water to last until the following day.

Buckets were stored in the washroom which the Benjamins used daily for bathing. The aayas boiled water on *choolas* (coal stoves), put some of the boiling water in the buckets and then topped up the buckets with a little cold water to create buckets of warm water. Each family member sat on a stool in the washroom and bathed him or herself using the warm water and some soap.

In later years, Hannah's brother Naji installed a small tank and showerhead in the washroom. However, the shower never worked properly as only cold water came in each evening through the mains, there was no element to heat the water and no water pressure.

The water pumped into Bombay homes wasn't suitable for drinking. In order to drink the water, the Benjamins strained it with a muslin-type cloth to remove sediment which collected in the water. Earthenware containers were often used in order to keep the drinking water cool in the hot Bombay temperatures. Although the water was chlorinated, it didn't contain fluoride, making it poor quality drinking water which caused many problems with the children's teeth.

Daily life in Bombay was therefore exceptionally labour intensive. Fortunately for Hannah, she had the help of her aayas.

The Aayas

Although the word *aaya* means 'maid' in Hindi, I never heard Nana, my father or any of my aunts or uncles use the word maid when describing their home help. They always translated the word *aayas* into English as the 'servants'.

I had an egalitarian upbringing and the thought that my grandparents had servants when they lived in India made me feel uncomfortable. I wondered what had happened to all the money my father's family had in Bombay: if they were so rich that they could afford home help in Bombay, what happened to all their wealth? It simply didn't make sense that my cost-conscious father could have grown up in a family with servants.

At the time, I didn't realise that aayas were commonplace in middle-class Bombay homes. The cost of labour in India was (and continues to be) so cheap that aayas simply weren't considered a luxury, nor were they a sign of wealth. Indeed, Hannah and Jacob – who lived quite a frugal existence by today's standards – employed not one, but two aayas. Similarly, most of the Baghdadi Jewish families in Bombay had aayas, even if they were part-time rather than live-in.

The Benjamins had the help of one aaya who came in the late afternoon every day and stayed until the evening. Her role was to wash the dishes and help tidy up after dinner. The second aaya actually lived with the Benjamin family. This live-in aaya's duties were to assist Hannah with cleaning, food preparation, washing dishes, shopping and heating water for bathing. In exchange for her work she received meals, board and a cash salary. The live-in changed often, but the other, a local Hindu woman named Dugree, stayed with the Benjamins for many years and they considered her part of their family.

Together, the two aayas helped Hannah with the more menial tasks around the Benjamins' home and they undoubtedly provided Hannah with a large degree of help. When I asked Nana whether she found looking after babies difficult, she quickly replied, 'No,' and added, 'it wasn't so hard.' She told me that her husband Jacob never helped her with the children, so I was surprised that she found looking after the children so easy.

Nana later admitted that the aayas helped her when the children were babies, particularly in the evenings by taking them out for walks. No wonder she didn't have such a difficult time looking after her children when they were young! (Although, to be fair, that may also be due to the expectations and mind-set she had as a mother; she wasn't, for example, trying to juggle motherhood with a career and she was a young woman when she had her children.)

Despite the help of the aayas, Hannah was very busy with cooking and other household chores.

Shopping, Cooking and Eating

Cooking for a family of eleven people plus an aaya – effectively twelve – is a time-consuming activity regardless of the era or country in which a family lives. But observing *kashrut* (the Jewish dietary laws) and with no refrigeration, food preparation required a lot of organisation, time and energy. Especially if you cooked the way Hannah Benjamin did.

Hannah's repertoire consisted of Iraqi, Indian and even British dishes. Her Iraqi specialties were *hamim*; *coobas*, both plain and the beetroot variety; and fish and meat *arookh* (stuffed fish/meat and rice cakes). Hannah cooked meat, chicken and fish curries, *bhajis*, *aloo* chops (rissoles filled with mince meat, potato and vegetables) and *dhal*. She also prepared meals like beef steak with vegetables.

Hannah made her own *amchur* (Indian spicy pickle) and her own jam, such as apricot and gooseberry jam. She baked English-style cakes like fruit cake, sponge cake and bread and butter pudding. She even made her own wine in big earthenware pots and her own vinegar.

My father recalls that there was always food in his parents' home. He is not one to freely give compliments, so I know that when he tells me that his mother 'cooked beautiful food', it must have been outstanding.

Hannah did all her cooking on the *choolas* (coal stoves). This was tricky as she couldn't control the temperature on the *choolas*. Around 1960, Hannah's brother Naji installed a portable gas cooker in place of the *choolas*, which meant Hannah was able to regulate the cooking temperature of her food for the first time. This, I imagine, would have made preparing meals significantly easier.

For most of Nana's years in Bombay, she did not have the use of a refrigerator. Without a fridge and with so many people to feed, Hannah was forced to buy fresh meat, fruit, vegetables and groceries every day, and extra on Friday to prepare for *Shabbat*, the only day on which she didn't cook. Food shopping and preparation took up a large amount of Hannah's time. With her depth of experience, however, she was very quick at preparing food and had usually finished her cooking by midday each day.

Given all the shopping she had to do, Hannah was lucky to live in Bombay where she didn't have to go far to buy ingredients for her cooking. She had street hawkers coming to her door to sell her the items she needed for her daily cooking, in a way I can only dream of today.

The fish sellers appeared at her door each morning selling pomfret, shouting '*sawa rupia joree*' – 'a rupee and a quarter for a pair of fresh pomfret'. '*Safed pani pomplate*', they announced, telling Hannah and other potential purchasers that their fish was fresh.

Sometimes they offered other seafood such as *bangra* (mackerel) or *jinga do anna plate* (a plate of prawns for the price of 2 annas). Of course, Hannah never bought the prawns as they're not kosher.

There were also the fruit vendors, the banana sellers and the *roti wallah* (flat-bread seller) who came selling *patla roti* (hot flat bread). And there was the *baida wallah* (egg seller) who came with a basket of eggs. '*Tootayla baida heh?*' ('Have you got cracked eggs?'), Hannah would ask him, as cracked eggs were always cheaper than intact ones. The children's favourite, unsurprisingly, was the ice-cream wallah, whose arrival they eagerly awaited.

Not all food items were brought to Hannah's doorstep for sale, but Hannah never had to go far if she needed to buy anything. Like many other Nagpada apartment blocks, the Benjamin family's apartment building was located above a series of shops. There was a greengrocer at the bottom of their building where Hannah could buy vegetables and across the street from the apartment were rice, sugar and bread shops. Spices were also easy to obtain from the local shops.

Hannah's sister Sarah remembers that Hannah and Jacob's neighbours had a much coveted fridge and Hannah occasionally used to go and ask them for a bottle of cold water – a much sought after luxury in Bombay's hot climate. Refrigerators were in short supply as not enough were being manufactured in India and most fridges were imported. In 1961, after waiting years to get a fridge under the quota system in place at the time in Bombay, Hannah did eventually get one. After all her years in Bombay without access to a refrigerator, Hannah no longer needed to buy fresh food on a daily basis. She would get to enjoy this luxury in Bombay for only five years before leaving for Australia.

Despite the volume and time-consuming nature of preparing food for such a large family, it seems that cooking was the simple part of Hannah's life. Looking after her children – even with the help of an aaya – proved challenging. Not only was there the round of expected childhood illnesses, but Hannah's children, particularly her boys, had a penchant for getting into mischief.

8. GROWING UP BENJAMIN: BOMBAY

I have grown up hearing my father's, aunts' and uncles' stories of their lives as children in Bombay. Their childhoods always sounded so carefree and so much more fun than mine. Imagine having eight brothers and sisters!

To be one of nine children must have been wonderful. To be the parents of nine children must have been wonderful as well, but also demanding, stressful and sometimes terrifying. Indeed, Hannah was a regular at the local hospital, with her children regularly getting sick or injuring themselves. Hannah's twin sister Sarah lived across the street from the Benjamins and laughed lovingly when she recounted to me how she was regularly called to take her twin sister's children to hospital. Sarah also frequently took care of her nieces and nephews when they were sick.

Hannah and Jacob's boys were particularly mischievous and I am sometimes amazed that the Benjamin children made it through their childhoods at all.

Illness and Injury

Mischief aside, the Benjamin children were struck with the usual round of childhood illnesses, which continued even into early adulthood.

Margaret and Elaine both got diphtheria; Margaret was often sick and actually contracted diphtheria a second time. She also got arsenic poisoning after being given the wrong injections. Florrie contracted typhoid when she was twenty-one years old and was so sick that she almost died. Hannah recalls that she only saw her husband Jacob cry twice in all the years she was married to him, and one of those times was when Florrie was sick with typhoid.

My father Abe had his share of sickness too. When he was only two years old, Abe poisoned himself by drinking some of Hannah's chloridine (a medicine used to stop diarrhoea). He had seen his mother drinking it and, as children do, he copied her. On returning home from synagogue on *Rosh Hashana* (Jewish New Year), Jacob noticed his son stumbling around and began to panic. Hannah realised that she had accidentally left the medicine bottle open and rushed Abe to the doctor, making sure to keep him awake. The doctor pumped out the little boy's stomach and Abe soon recovered. I expect it took his parents slightly longer to recover from the experience.

When he was nine years old, Abe had his tonsils removed. Only days later, he developed appendicitis and had to have his appendix out. And then when he was seventeen, Abe was in hospital with hepatitis for one week and almost died.

Many of the Benjamin children's illnesses were unavoidable. But in addition to childhood diseases, the Benjamin boys brought injuries upon themselves. For example, when Abe was seven years old, he put a tamarind seed up his nose, only to find it went further up his nose when he tried to get it out. Abe had to be taken to hospital where the seed had to be removed with tweezers. His mother was not impressed.

However, there was one particular escapade of my father's childhood which had more lasting effects. During the Hindu festival of *Diwali* (the Festival of Lights), the local Byculla Hindus used to light firecrackers each day and night. With firecrackers being inexpensive and easy to obtain during *Diwali* from the multitude of firecracker shops, Abe, his brothers and their friends used to buy and play with firecrackers. For pure amusement, they lit 'bombs' or 'bungers' and covered the crackers with tin cans and buckets, causing the cans and buckets to fly very high when the firecrackers exploded.

One afternoon when Abe was around ten years old, he was trying to light a 'bunger' but it didn't ignite. This occasionally happened, but the boys never threw the dud firecrackers out as they didn't want to waste them. Instead, they cut the cardboard firecracker open to expose the gunpowder and wick, and then ignited the gunpowder and wick with a match or a sparkler.

That particular time, Abe was the one to remove the cardboard casing from the firecracker. But before he could move his hands out of the way, one of the older boys lit a sparkler and set the gunpowder alight. Abe's hands, still right next to the gunpowder, were completely burnt. He was in agony after the explosion and even now, over fifty years later, his left thumb is still scarred and out of shape as a result of the burn.

Abe was terrified of showing his mother as he knew that he'd 'get a spanking from her', So he hid his burnt, throbbing hands behind his back as he tried to sneak home quietly to try and quickly cool his hands under cold water. But Abe could not outsmart his mother.

Unsurprisingly, in such a small community everyone knew each other's business and there were few secrets. So Hannah already knew what had happened to her son; one of the neighbours had witnessed the whole incident and reported it to Hannah. Hannah had to take Abe to hospital – again. It took many weeks for Abe's blistered skin to heal and he clearly remembers that during this time, he had to go to the school dispensary every day to have his wounds dressed.

But it was Sass who was the most mischievous of the five brothers. Hannah told me that when Sass was young, she never used to leave him alone in the house as she was scared he'd 'throw himself or burn himself'. Hannah was constantly in and out of hospital with Sass and told me that of all her children, only he gave her big trouble.

Despite (or perhaps because of) the gravity of some of their antics, the Benjamin brothers love telling stories of their childhood. When they're in storytelling mode, they're transformed from middle-aged men who know how difficult life can be, to young boys with a not a care in the world who think that no harm can befall them.

Abe recalls his childhood being a happy one. It was impossible for Hannah and Jacob to closely monitor the activities of their many children. Instead – as in other large families – the siblings helped looked after each other.

The Benjamin children were free to live their lives and to play with each other and their friends with minimal parental interference. Many of the hours before and after school were theirs to do with as they chose.

As a young schoolboy, Abe ate breakfast each morning with his brothers and sisters. The aaya prepared breakfast supplies in advance and put them on the table so the children could help themselves to tea, hot milk, bread, butter and jam. Hannah would usually help, making sure her children sat down and ate before they went to school for the day.

The Sir Jacob Sassoon School was only a two-minute walk from the Benjamins' apartment and sometimes Abe met friends in the school grounds to play before classes started at 9.30 a.m. After school finished at 4.00 p.m. Abe went home for a quick bath and cup of *chai* (tea) – prepared by the aaya – before going outside or back to the school grounds to meet friends and play. Bombay was permanently warm and it stayed light until late, so other than at monsoon time from mid-June to mid-September, the weather was conducive to outdoor play. The Benjamins rarely ate dinner before 8.00 p.m. so there was lots of time for the children to amuse themselves in the late afternoon and early evening.

There wasn't much space to play inside the Benjamins' tiny apartment, so my father and his siblings usually played on the street with their friends. With few toys and no television, they made do with whatever – and whomever – they could find to entertain themselves. What they lacked in terms of possessions, they made up for in friendship and companionship.

Like other Indian boys, the Benjamin boys' favourite game was cricket, but they also played *gilly dan do* (known in English as 'tip cat') and games with empty cigarette packets, bottle caps, marbles and tops. Occasionally they played cards at home. Abe also loved to climb coconut palms in the school grounds and pick coconuts off them.

The most fun and entertainment, however, was provided when the boys incorporated unsuspecting passers-by into their games.

Watermelon skins were one of the boys' favourite ways of causing havoc with the locals. To cool themselves down in the Bombay heat and humidity, the Iranian owners of a nearby restaurant used to cut watermelons in half, scoop out the flesh and put the cool watermelon skins on their heads. Those same apparently harmless watermelon skins were used by the Benjamin brothers for their own entertainment.

The boys tied string to the discarded watermelon skins and left them aside until night time. After dark, they switched off their apartment lights and lay on their mattresses on the floor of their home. Then, they threw the heavy green skins over the branches of the large trees opposite their apartment, while at the same time holding onto the string at the other end.

As people walked past, the boys would let the strings down so that the skins thumped the passers-by on the head. Before the bewildered passers-by could work out what was going on, the boys would quickly pull the strings up again.

My father, well and truly middle-aged by the time he told me this story, laughed like a boy when he remembered one particular victim. This man stood around for ages trying to work out what was going on as watermelon skin after watermelon skin tapped him on the head, unable to solve the mystery due to the darkened apartment from where the boys operated.

Another of the Benjamin boys' favourite games was to take *pice* (coins: this was before decimalisation and 4 pice made 1 anna; 16 annas made a rupee) and push them into the tar on the roads, which had softened in the summer heat. Once pushed in, the boys would run away and watch the passers-by try to pick up the coins, laughing hysterically as they were unable to dislodge the pice despite their best efforts.

The local fruit-sellers also fell victim to the mischievous boys. As the vendors walked by carrying baskets full of fruit on their heads, the boys would help themselves to fruit without the sellers noticing.

Even the local musicians were targeted. These musicians often came by to play music at wedding receptions, blowing their tubas and trumpets. One time, one of the neighbour's boys told Sammy Benjamin to sit on the boundary wall and watch the band playing. He was to take a lime, squeeze it in his mouth and pretend he was sucking on it while the band played. This made the band members salivate which in turn caused their music to be out of tune. Furious that this young boy had disrupted their performance, they came and chased Sammy, but he quickly jumped off the wall before they could catch him.

As they grew older, Abe, his brothers and friends found less intrusive forms of entertainment. They often went out together on Saturday evenings after *Shabbat*. They mostly went to Chowpatty Beach for Indian snacks like *chat patay*, or to the movies. On Sunday nights they sometimes caught a bus to Pasta Lane or the waterfront area of Apollo Bunda near the Taj Hotel for a boat ride or simply to socialise with friends, just to get out in the evening and 'kill some hours'. During the week they sometimes went to the movies too, a very popular pastime in India even today.

Abe and his friends also went swimming at Back Bay Baths, which was located in the Colaba area of Bombay. The Jewish sporting organisation Maccabi used to rent the saltwater pool at Back Bay Baths for about an hour each evening, and Abe and his friends often caught a bus there to have a swim.

None of the Benjamin children had formal swimming lessons. Rather, they taught themselves to swim, using empty oil cans to help keep themselves above water. In order to convert the oil cans into flotation devices, they soldered the opening shut to seal the can and added a hook to thread string through. They then tied the oil can to their backs with string or rope to help keep themselves afloat.

That was the 1940s and '50s, decades in which Jewish children in Europe were, if not robbed of their lives, then certainly robbed of their childhoods. How blessed the Benjamins were to be living in Bombay. Life for the them may have been challenging at times, but it was essentially uncomplicated, enjoyable and safe.

Abe at Juhu Beach,
Bombay, 1965

9. JEWISH LIFE

Had Hannah and Jacob Benjamin been European Jews and not Jews of India, they would never have been able to have the number of children they did over the same period of time. If not for this chance of history, I probably would not be here today.

In April 1943, my grandmother Hannah was pregnant with my father Abe. At the exact same time in the Warsaw Ghetto, Polish Jews were staging an uprising against their Nazi persecutors. The Warsaw Ghetto Uprising was an act of tremendous bravery and courage. Yet it saw thousands of Jews killed and most of the survivors shipped to death camps.

It is truly incredible to contrast the persecution and mass murder of Europe's Jews by the Nazis in the 1930s and '40s with India's Jews' ability to practise their religion freely and without fear of discrimination. Indeed, the Jewish communities of India have the unique distinction of never having being victimised by anti-Semitism by Indian rulers or the Indian population.[24] (That comment predates the horrific attack on the Nariman House Jewish Community Centre which killed six people during the 2008 Mumbai terrorist attacks, but even that incident has been attributed to Pakistani rather than Indian nationals.)

As a result of this religious freedom, the Jewish communities of India thrived. Judaism was not simply a religion; rather, it was an integral component of the daily lives of the Baghdadi Jews. Although the members of the Benjamin family were not strictly observant, they wholly identified as Jews.

Hannah and Jacob brought their children up in a traditional

Jewish home. They ensured each child learned to read Hebrew and knew the prayer tunes and customs of the Baghdadi Jews. Having been taught by her father, Hannah shared her knowledge with her children. She taught by example too – she was charitable and always gave leftovers to the poor who went from door to door every evening soliciting food.

Each week, the Benjamin family celebrated *Shabbat*. They also celebrated all the *chagim* (festivals) which punctuate the Jewish calendar. The Benjamins and the wider Baghdadi community had some interesting practices and rituals. Some of their Iraqi customs have been retained; others have evolved to take into account the fact that the community has dissolved and dispersed around the globe. As always, food was a central component of the way in which each of the Jewish holidays was observed in Bombay.

Shabbat

Shabbat is the day of rest for the Jewish people, when all work is prohibited. It is the culmination of the Jewish week, beginning at sundown on Friday and finishing when three stars appear in the sky on Saturday evening. The *halacha* (Jewish law) regarding *Shabbat* observance never changes. However, in each generation and within each community, and even from one family to another, different customs and rituals are followed to celebrate *Shabbat*.

The commencement of *Shabbat* is marked by the lighting of at least two candles by the women of each Jewish household. In my home and in my mother's home, we light white candles which sit in special *Shabbat* candlesticks. But in Bombay, the Jewish women did not use candles. Rather, Hannah and the other women in her family and community lit seven floating wicks in the hanging *triyah*.

The *triyah* consisted of seven small glasses filled with coconut oil and water, with wicks floating on top of the oil and water mixture. Hannah made the *fittel*, the wicks for the oil, herself. The *triyah* sat in a brass chandelier and this chandelier hung from the ceiling of the Benjamins' apartment. Each week, Hannah stood on a chair and lit each of the seven wicks to usher in *Shabbat*. The lighting of the *triyah* is one custom that the Baghdadi Jews did not bring with them when they left Bombay; I have never seen a *triyah* outside of India.

After candle lighting, but prior to eating the special *Shabbat* meal, blessings over wine (*kiddush*) and bread (*hamotzi*) are made. After India gained independence from Britain in 1947, wine became prohibited in India. So Hannah made her own non-alcoholic wine each week by soaking blackcurrants in water and then boiling the blackcurrant-infused water. Once boiled, she left the liquid to stand until it thickened and then used this for *kiddush* wine. As for bread, in Bombay, *hamotzi* was made not on the *challah* (plaited egg loaf) that I have grown up eating, but on *patla roti*, a thin, almost unleavened bread.

Friday night dinner was always special in the Benjamin household. The dining table was moved from its usual place against the wall into the centre of the room and covered with a tablecloth. The entire family sat together and ate the special meal which Hannah had prepared, usually soup, *hamim*, *coobas* and her specialty, *aloomakalas* (the same 'jumping potatoes' she made for her children and grandchildren many years later when she moved to Sydney). Often, Jacob bought beer especially for *Shabbat* in order to make his children shandies – beer mixed with lemonade – to drink.

It is customary to have guests on *Shabbat*, and Jacob's mother Habiba and brother Salem usually joined the Benjamins for Friday night dinner. Habiba often bought watermelon and always saved the seeds (*garinim* in Hebrew, *hub* in Arabic) which she later dried, roasted and salted. She always arrived at Hannah and Jacob's for Friday night dinner with her pockets full of *garinim* for her adored grandchildren.

After dinner, Abe was often joined by friends who came to his apartment and walked with him to the Synagogue Compound. There, an *Oneg Shabbat* (celebration of *Shabbat*) was held with many community members celebrating by socialising and singing.

Most of the men and even the boys in the community – including my grandfather Jacob and my father Abe – went to synagogue on Friday evenings. The synagogue easily accommodated 500 people and although it didn't have a rabbi, it did have a cantor. However, it was difficult for some Bombay Jews to observe *Shabbat* due to their work commitments in line with the six-day working week in India. As a result, only some 100–200 people attended Saturday morning services.

Due to the Bombay heat, the Saturday morning service started very early, at 6.15 a.m. but finished by 9.00 a.m. (in contrast, the synagogue I attend in Sydney doesn't even start until 10.00 a.m. on a Saturday!) Abe remembers that if he looked out the window of his apartment on a Saturday morning, he could see Jewish men, women and children from the surrounding Byculla streets walking towards the Synagogue. When the service concluded later that morning, he could see them all walking home. It was an amazing sight.

My father has always loved *Shabbat*. Although both his parents rarely went to synagogue on Saturday mornings, Abe regularly attended morning synagogue services and afternoon activities at his youth group, Bnei Akiva. Today in Sydney, my father strictly observes the Jewish day of rest.

The Jewish Holidays

Each of the *chagim* evokes its own sounds, smells and feelings. For me, the change of weather from summer to autumn in Sydney always signals that *Pesach* (Passover) is in the air. Similarly, the beginning of spring is *Rosh Hashana* (Jewish New Year) weather. Quite simply, although they require a lot of preparation, I love the

Jewish holidays. They are a time for spiritual reflection, personal growth and time spent with family and friends. So too, my father's memories of his years in Bombay are synchronised with the cyclical nature of the Jewish year.

Purim was one of the favourite festivals of the Baghdadi community's children. As is customary, the children wore fancy dress and people exchanged *mishloach manot* (food parcels) with their families, friends and neighbours. Today, *hamantaschen*, the triangular-shaped biscuits filled with jam, poppy seeds (or in my family, dates) are eaten in many Jewish communities on *Purim*.

However, baking and eating *hamantaschen* is not a custom of India's Baghdadi Jews. Rather, the women of the community prepared all kinds of Indian sweets such as *loozina* (literally 'diamond-shaped'). All different flavoured *loozina* were made, such as coconut *loozina* and almond *loozina*. The Baghdadi Jews of Bombay also baked *kakas* (ring-shaped biscuits), *babas* (biscuits filled with dates), marzipan biscuits and carrot *halva*.

For the Benjamin children, *Purim* was a particularly special holiday which they eagerly anticipated. Every year, on *Purim* afternoon, Hannah, Jacob, their children and Jacob's mother Habiba went to Jacob's Uncle Isaac and Aunty Helen's home (Isaac was one of the two uncles with whom Jacob had fled Baghdad for Bombay).

Isaac was the Chief Engineer of the Jacob Mills and he and his wife Helen actually lived on-site. The Jacob Mills produced cotton and were owned by the Sassoons; when the Sassoons sold them in the 1950s, they were renamed the India United Mills. There was a tennis court in the grounds of the Mills and a large area in which the children could run around and play. Unsurprisingly, the Benjamin children loved to go to their Uncle Isaac and Aunty Helen's home.

Every *Purim*, Nani Habiba arrived at Hannah and Jacob's home by 11.00 a.m., all dressed and ready to go, even though the family wouldn't be leaving for another few hours and the Mills were not far away. When they finally arrived in the early afternoon, the Benjamin children played with their cousins; Jacob, his brothers and friends played cards, and the women chatted and sometimes joined the card games. Of course, there were the obligatory snacks and *chai* (tea), before they left long after nightfall.

It was traditional for the adults to give the children *Purim* money, just as my aunts and uncles gave me money for *Purim* when I was a child. The Benjamin children knew exactly which of their relatives to approach for the biggest contribution. Jacob's brother Salem was particularly generous with his nieces and nephews. All my father Abe had to say was, 'Hi Uncle Salem, how you doing?' and Salem would reply, 'Here, take 4 annas.' By the time the children had collected their spoils from their Uncle Salem and Aunties Helen and Ella, they would go home with 20 rupees each. Quite a windfall in those days, which my father and his siblings promptly proceeded to spend at the local shops.

Almost as soon as *Purim* was over, work began to build a *matza* oven at the back of the Magen David Synagogue in Byculla. During the eight-day festival of *Pesach*, Jews are prohibited from eating bread and other products made with leaven, and instead eat an unleavened bread called *matza*. Funded by the Sassoon Trust, the Jewish community organised the baking of their own *matzot*. Unlike the mass-produced variety sold in supermarkets today, the Bombay *matzot* were hand-made and baked in the purpose-built *matza* oven. And every year at the conclusion of *Pesach*, the *matza* oven was dismantled.

The boxed *matza* which I buy today is almost cracker-like in texture. But my father remembers wetting the Bombay *matzot* in order to make them more pliable and rolling *shiftas* (meat patties) in them. The Baghdadi Jews also ate *matza* with *halek*, a date syrup mixed with crushed nuts. Hannah made her own *halek* for Pesach, just as my father does in Sydney today. It is a laborious activity which involves soaking dates in water overnight, squeezing out the saturated dates, then boiling the resulting liquid to make a syrup. The effort, however, is worthwhile as *halek* is absolutely delicious and one of the few saving graces in having to abstain from eating bread and other leavened staples for eight days in a row.

After *Pesach* comes *Shavuot*, then *Rosh Hashana*. For this festival, Hannah and the other Baghdadi Jewish women cooked apple jam, a traditional Iraqi delicacy which is eaten to signify the hope that the year ahead will be a sweet one (Ashkenazi communities customarily eat pieces of apple dipped in honey.)

On *Rosh Hashana*, Jacob Benjamin held the honour of blowing the *shofar* (ram's horn) for the congregation in the Magen David Synagogue, having been taught to do so by his grandfather *Chacham* Avraham. Today, it is Jacob's son Sammy who blows the *shofar* in Sydney's Sephardi Synagogue. The *shofar* which Uncle Sammy blows is identical to the one his father used and was given to Sammy by his Uncle Isaac in Bombay. Both Jacob and Sammy Benjamin's *shofars* originate from Baghdad and were sent to Bombay from Baghdad over eighty years ago.

On both *Rosh Hashana* and *Yom Kippur* (the Day of Atonement, which is the holiest day of the Jewish year and obliges Jews to fast for twenty-five hours), the Magen David Synagogue was filled to capacity and all of its chandeliers lit. It was a spectacular sight, particularly on *Yom Kippur* against the backdrop of an entire congregation dressed in customary white.

My father remembers that some people – those who didn't live as close to the Synagogue as the Benjamins – used to bring their mattresses and sleep there in the rooms above the Synagogue, or even outdoors in the Synagogue grounds, so that they didn't have to go home at night and come back the next morning. After the fast ended, some of the older children took the *garry gora* (horse and buggy) to Chowpatty Beach, where they feasted on ice-cream or *bhel puri* (fried crisp wheat cakes crushed up with puffed rice, pea flour noodles, coriander leaf and spices), celebrating the end of another year's fast.

Yom Kippur was followed by *Succot* and *Simchat Torah*. The last of the Jewish holidays in the calendar year is *Chanukah*, the eight-day so-called Festival of Lights. When my father lights the *chanukiah* (candle holder) each year, he sings the Iraqi tune to the psalm *Mizmor Shir Chanukat Habayit*. My husband's Ashkenazi *siddur* (prayer book) instructs that this psalm is to be read in synagogue, but the Baghdadi custom has always been to sing it after lighting the *Chanukah* candles at home.

I have loved the tune of this psalm since I was a child and know that when my father sings it each *Chanukah*, it takes him back to his Bombay childhood. It was a childhood permeated by Judaism and the traditions of his Iraqi ancestors, and a childhood which was also quite insulated from the wider Indian society in which he lived.

10. THE BAGHDADIS AND THE BRITISH

Of the three Jewish communities in India (Baghdadis, Bene Israel and Cochinis), it was the Baghdadi Jews who were the least assimilated into Indian culture. The Bene Israel and Cochin Jews identified with their local Indian communities. In contrast, although the Baghdadi Jews lived in harmony with their Indian neighbours, they kept themselves apart from their host community.

My father Abe did play with the non-Jewish children who lived in his apartment building from time to time, but he didn't really have any non-Jewish friends. Socialising with non-Jewish children wasn't encouraged and Abe and his siblings didn't really mix with the local Indian community.

Indeed, prior to India's independence from Britain, India's Baghdadi Jews tended to align themselves with the British rulers of India rather than with the Indian population. This led to the Baghdadi Jews speaking English in place of their native Arabic and wearing Western clothing rather than traditional Iraqi clothing.

The emotional embodiment of the shift from Baghdadi to British identity was the death in Baghdad of *Chacham* Joseph Hayyim in 1909, the last of the great leaders of Iraqi Jewry. Indian Baghdadis had looked to him for spiritual and legal advice for decades, but he had no successor. The Baghdadi Jews of India subsequently shifted their locus of religious authority from Baghdad to London's chief rabbi.[25]

Language and Clothing

Historically, the mother tongue of the Baghdadi Jews was Arabic. They spoke Arabic in their homes for generations and Judeo-Arabic (Arabic written in the Hebrew alphabet) was used for written purposes, in newspapers and correspondence with Jewish communities elsewhere.[26] Hebrew was the language used for all learning and ritual observance.[27]

However, as part of the Baghdadi Jews' process of identification with British culture, they began to adopt English as their first language. During the 20th century, English overtook Arabic as the first language in most Baghdadi Jewish homes. At the same time, the Baghdadi Jews spoke Hindustani in the kitchen, on the street and often when talking among themselves, especially during the last quarter of the 19th century.

This historical shift from Arabic to English, while also speaking Hindustani, is consistent with the experience of the Benjamin family. Between my great-grandparents' and my father's generation, the Benjamins shifted from being primarily Arabic speakers to using English as their first language.

My great-grandmother Habiba's first language was Arabic. She was, however, also able to speak English as she'd been schooled in British-ruled Bombay for a number of years when she was a child.

One generation later, things were already beginning to change. Although both Hannah and Jacob could speak and write in Arabic, having learnt it from their parents, their first language was English. As a child, Hannah spoke English at school and to her siblings at home, although she tended to use Arabic with her parents. After she married Jacob, English continued to be Hannah's preferred language, but she and Jacob sometimes used a bit of Arabic between themselves in conversation. At the same time, Hannah spoke Hindustani in the shops as all the shopkeepers were Indian.

Interestingly, the eldest of the Benjamin children, Florrie, remembers Arabic being spoken at home more than my sixth-born father does. Florrie always conversed with her Nani Habiba in Arabic. In comparison, Habiba spoke to Abe in Arabic and Hindustani, but Abe answered her only in English or Hindustani, never in Arabic.

There was a marked decline in the use of Arabic within the Benjamin family as the years went by. By the time my father was born, the Benjamin family rarely spoke anything other than English at home. Jacob's mother Habiba was keen to keep up with this move to English and was very proud of her ability to speak English like the younger generations. Florrie fondly remembers Habiba checking her English spelling with her grandchildren for basic words like 'the', 'cat', 'dog' and 'it'. And Abe recalls his Nani Habiba picking up English newspapers and reading from them, albeit slowly. 'Am I reading English correctly?' she would ask her grandson.

Although Habiba attempted to keep up with the shift in language from Arabic to English, she continued to wear traditional Iraqi clothing. In comparison, by the 1940s and '50s in Bombay, the Baghdadi Jewish men and younger Baghdadi women had already adopted British attire in place of traditional Iraqi clothing. Jacob Benjamin always wore Western clothing and even Hannah's father Sassoon wore pants and a jacket to synagogue as early as the 1920s.

However, the older Baghdadi women – including my great-grandmothers Habiba and Aziza – continued to wear more traditional clothing such as the *lapar* and *chadar*. *Lapar* is an Arabic word used to describe the long, flowing gown worn by women in various colours which reached their ankles and was sometimes used to cover their heads. The *chadar*, a white cloak which covered the wearer's head but not face, was sometimes worn over the *lapar*.

Admittedly, in later years, Habiba stopped wearing the *chadar* and started wearing long robes and shawls (had Aziza lived longer, she may have done so too but she died in 1948). But my grandmother Hannah never wore the *chadar*. Rather, she wore long gowns in her home and added a shawl to her outfit when going outside her apartment. One generation later, Hannah's daughters only ever wore Western clothing in Bombay.

By the time they left Bombay in the late 1950s and early 1960s, the way the Benjamins dressed and the language they spoke showed little connection to their Iraqi roots.

Today, the descendants of the Baghdadi Jews of Bombay are almost completely Westernised. I would venture to say that none of Hannah and Jacob's grandchildren can speak more than a few words of Arabic (although all of us understand the word *inshallah* – 'God willing', often invoked by our parents, aunts and uncles when bestowing good wishes on us for health, wealth, marriage and children). The most exposure I've ever had to Arabic was hearing Nana reciting parts of the *Pesach* (Passover) *Seder* in Arabic in my parents' home each year.

The majority of Hannah and Jacob's grandchildren are monolingual and if any of us do speak a second language, it is probably Hebrew. Rather than Arabic, we are more likely to understand and speak some Hindustani words and phrases.

Sadly, Jacob Benjamin never got to speak to any of his grandchildren in Arabic, or in Hindustani, or in English. While Hannah lived to see all of her grandchildren and many of her great-grandchildren, Jacob did not live to see even one of them. My own father was only a boy himself when his father died. Abe felt the loss of his father deeply, particularly since Jacob's death occurred only just before my father's barmitzvah (coming of age ceremony when a Jewish boy turns thirteen years old and is considered to be an adult).

11. 'PAPA' JACOB

Jacob Benjamin knew that he was dying. Not at first. But towards the end of his life, Jacob admitted to his eldest daughter Florrie that he didn't think he would live to see her marry the following year, despite his previous promises that he would be with her under the *chuppah*. He also confessed to her that he didn't think he would live to see his first grandchild, whose birth was only months away.

In March 1956, Jacob Benjamin was diagnosed with cancer of the tonsils. The years preceding his diagnosis had not been easy ones for him. In 1949, at forty-seven years old, Jacob had suffered a heart attack. Not long before this heart attack, Jacob had lost his life savings after a business venture turned sour.

It was not unusual for Jews and Muslims in Bombay to have business dealings with each other. After being retrenched from his job as a clerk in the E. D. Sassoon Mills, Jacob decided to invest his money in the building of billiard tables. He found a business partner, a Muslim man, and the two ran a billiard salon where they owned all the tables. However, Jacob lost all his money, including his Provident Fund (basically all his retirement savings) after his business partner cheated him. Heart trouble runs in the Benjamin family and Jacob was a cigarette smoker (although he did give up smoking after the heart attack), but it seems likely that the stress of the failed business contributed to his heart attack.

Jacob survived the heart attack and after he recovered he tried his hand at a completely different business: leasing premises in Byculla and running a kosher butcher shop. However, running the local butcher was not an easy way to make a living. Due to the lack of proper refrigeration, only enough animals for a day's supply of meat were slaughtered. This meant that Jacob had to attend the daily slaughterings each evening, after waking up at 4.00 a.m. each morning for work. It was physically exhausting and became quite a strain on him. It wasn't long before Jacob started feeling unwell again and he subsequently gave up the business due to ill health. All in all, he ran the kosher butcher shop for less than a year.

Jacob didn't know what was making him feel unwell but he knew something was amiss. Margaret was the first of Hannah and Jacob's children to get married, in February 1956. Although this was a great family *simcha* (joyous event), the state of Jacob's health cast a shadow over the celebrations. Soon after Margaret's wedding, Jacob began to complain of a sore throat and started coughing every morning.

It was only seven months between the cancer diagnosis and Jacob's death. Jacob did receive radiation treatment, but it wasn't successful and he suffered considerable pain. During his illness, Jacob would wait for Florrie to come home from work each evening and ask her to tell him what she had done that day. Florrie would hold his hand, sit with him and answer his questions. But she found the nightly ritual emotionally draining. She knew that her father, who she simply adored, was dying.

My father was only twelve years old at the time and his memories of his father's illness are vague. Yet Abe clearly recalls a particular Saturday when he and his brother Sammy had gone to the cinema. When they returned home the doctor was with their father. Later that day, the doctor transferred Jacob to hospital. Abe never saw his father again.

Jacob didn't survive for even a week in hospital. On the morning of Thursday 18 October 1956, Jacob Benjamin passed away. He was only fifty-four years old.

Although there was a *Chevra Kadisha* (Jewish burial society) in Bombay, purification of Jacob's body before burial was carried out in the Benjamins' apartment by members of the Baghdadi Jewish community. Those same community members stayed with Jacob's body at Hannah and Jacob's home until Jacob's burial, which took place later that Thursday afternoon. (Jewish law dictates that burial must occur as soon as possible after death and that the body of the deceased must not be left alone in the intervening period.)

Both Hannah and Abe were precluded from attending Jacob's funeral. The practice at the time was that females did not go to the cemetery for funerals. Instead, women went to the cemetery on the third day after burial. Nana's grief was so great that when she was finally permitted to go to the cemetery on the third day, she threw herself on Jacob's grave in sorrow.

As for my father, as a male he was technically permitted to attend his father's funeral. But Hannah's sister Sarah and brother Naji decided that twelve-year-old Abe was too young to be present at the funeral, even though he wanted to go. I am certain that my great-aunt and great-uncle were trying to protect my father by not allowing him to attend. But to this day, Abe regrets that he wasn't present to bury his father.

Jacob's death was a tragedy for the Benjamin family. It left Hannah a widow and their nine children fatherless. At the time Jacob died, eight of Hannah and Jacob's children were still living at home. Isaac, the youngest, was only three years old. Jacob's death also left his mother Habiba with only three of her original five children still alive. Habiba actually outlived another of her sons a few years after Jacob's death. Her grief in outliving not one, but three, of her children must have been utterly devastating.

Jacob's death was therefore untimely in many ways. Sadly, his death also took place only one month before his first grandchild, Margaret's daughter, was born. And as he predicted, Jacob didn't survive to see his eldest daughter Florrie marry.

The tragedy of Jacob's death was compounded by the fact that he left his wife Hannah without money and also in debt. At the time Jacob died there was five months rent outstanding on their apartment, and Hannah described herself as an 'absolute pauper' after her husband's death.

When my father Abe had been born more than ten years earlier in 1943, the Benjamins were in quite a comfortable financial position. But by the time Jacob was diagnosed with cancer he didn't have a proper job and he died utterly penniless. Hannah couldn't even afford to pay for Jacob's tombstone until Jacob's uncle Moses sent money from the US which Hannah used for this purpose. Jacob's actual burial was free so at least Hannah didn't have to pay for that.

In order to survive, Hannah was forced to rely on financial support provided by her very generous brother Naji. She also received some financial assistance from the Jewish community.

Naji was a qualified engineer but he made his money by manufacturing cleaning powder (similar to today's Ajax) and selling it to shops. Naji wasn't wealthy, but he was a generous man with a good heart. He helped Hannah enormously: he gave her an allowance and also gave her money with which to buy clothes, books and other items which her children needed. Without Naji's help, I am not sure what my grandmother would have done.

My father's thirteenth birthday on the Jewish calendar – his bar mitzvah – was just five weeks after Jacob's death. For the Baghdadi Jews, the occasion of a boy's bar mitzvah is marked by the boy putting on *tefillin* (phylacteries) for the first time. In Sydney, the tradition has evolved to include the bar mitzvah boy reading from the Torah, but my father had already done that when he was just seven years old.

Bar mitzvahs are significant life cycle events for Jewish boys and are almost always accompanied by family celebrations. Indeed, the bar mitzvahs of all four of Abe's brothers were celebrated by the

Benjamin family with parties at home, accompanied by cakes and *machbooz* (Iraqi baked goods) that their mother had prepared.

But with the loss of Jacob still so fresh, my father's bar mitzvah was literally forgotten. No party was organised by Hannah and neither she nor any of Abe's uncles, or even his religious grandmother Habiba, arranged for someone to help Abe to put on his *tefillin*, which is initially a difficult task. In fact, on the day of my father's thirteenth birthday, his brother Sammy and sister Mabel left for camp!

But Abe knew it was time for him to start wearing *tefillin*. So on the morning of his bar mitzvah, he simply went to synagogue on his own and had the *chazan* (cantor) show him how to put on *tefillin*. This no fuss approach is so typical of my father that I am not at all surprised, and he has religiously put on his *tefillin* every day since (except on *Shabbat* and other times it is not required).

Rather than feeling guilty that she had neglected the occasion, Hannah was annoyed at her son. Abe, she told me, should have told his uncles that he wanted to wear his *tefillin* on his *barmiswa* (this interchanging of the 'v' and 'w' sounds in English is a hallmark of the Baghdadi Jews, and indeed, of many Indians). By putting on his *tefillin* without a family member present, Abe had failed to give Jacob's brothers – his uncles – the honour of helping him.

Of course, such an honour would have belonged to Jacob had he been alive. On that day, as on other momentous days in his life, my father acutely felt the loss of his father Jacob. He knew that had his father been alive, his bar mitzvah would have been an entirely different event.

I have visited Jacob Benjamin's grave site only once in my life. That was in February 2003, on my first trip to India. During the four weeks in which my father, my brother, my husband and I travelled through India, the five days we spent in Mumbai were undoubtedly the highlight. With my father Abe as our guide, we visited Mumbai's major tourist attractions. More importantly, I spent time in the neighbourhood in which some of my great-grandparents, all of my grandparents and both my parents used to live. It was an incredible experience.

PART 2

MUMBAI, 2003

12. FIRST IMPRESSIONS

As I sat in the airport lounge in the south Indian city of Bangalore waiting to board my flight to Mumbai, I felt a mixture of apprehension and excitement. I knew that Mumbai would be different to the Bombay I'd been told about all my life, yet I still had a sense that I was going to a city to which I somehow belonged. A city to which I was, and still am, deeply connected. Even though I am Australian-born, there is part of me that feels like India is my country of origin. And in a way it is: for one-and-a-half to two generations before mine, both my mother's and father's families lived in India.

I had been travelling with my father, brother and husband in India's south before arriving in Bangalore and we had met two acquaintances from home. Those Sydneysiders hadn't tolerated more than two days of Mumbai's beggars and hawkers, and they left for Goa much earlier than planned. Before I left Sydney, my mother had warned me about the filth and poverty prevalent in Mumbai. It was not at all the city she remembered from her youth. I wondered whether it was possible that I would dislike the city which I had felt drawn to for so many years.

An announcement of which I didn't understand the meaning, but recognised as Hindi, suddenly interrupted my thoughts. Then, the translation in heavily Indian-accented English: Jet Airways flight to Mumbai was boarding and we were to proceed for a security check.

I joined the female-only queue for the mandatory pre-flight frisk by an unsmiling Indian woman. I met up with my father, brother and husband on the tarmac and took a deep breath. On an otherwise unremarkable sunny, Friday afternoon in February 2003, I was at last going to Mumbai.

It occurred to me that at this time on a Friday some fifty, sixty or seventy years ago, my parents and grandparents would not have been travelling anywhere, except maybe home from work. Instead, they would have been busy preparing for *Shabbat*. They would have been rushing to cook, clean, bathe and have their table set before *Shabbat* began.

My brother was sitting next to me on the plane and pointed out an article which appeared in the glossy in-flight magazine, *Jetwings*. It was titled 'Memories of Matheran'. The article read: 'Fed up of Mumbai? Who isn't, at times? Leave urban angst and motor cars behind and head for the nearest hill station. Matheran offers fresh air, panoramic views – and monkeys.' The text was accompanied by a photograph of a seven-carriage train winding up through incredibly lush green hills. Its caption read: 'Going round the bend? Take the toy train for a weekend in Matheran.'

My brother and I giggled in unison. We have heard countless stories about camps my father and his brothers and sisters went on in what they pronounced 'Matran' and their adventures on the 'toy train'. (Matheran is 110 kilometres from Mumbai and to travel there by rail you take a train from Mumbai and then change and catch the toy train for the last 21 kilometres to Matheran.)

It was strange to see pictures of a place I had only ever visualised in my mind. My father never mentioned the beauty and apparent serenity of Matheran. I tried to visualise my father and his friends on the toy train, before they had wives and husbands and children of their own. I could not imagine it.

As I flicked through the remaining articles, I realised we had begun our descent into Mumbai. I peered with curiosity out the window but was unable to make out any detail in the land mass below me. My father, however, knew exactly what lay beneath the smog-infested sky. He excitedly pointed out key landmarks to us: Mumbai's city centre, Chowpatty Beach and the Gateway of India. It struck me as strange that the geography of this city was so familiar to my father even though it had been thirty-seven years since he'd lived in Mumbai, yet completely foreign to me. It was a reminder that although I am a central part of my parents' lives, they once existed completely free of me.

As soon as our plane touched down, my father grinned excitedly. 'Welcome to Mumbai,' he greeted us, almost as if we were his guests. I asked him whether Mumbai felt at all like home to him. 'No,' he replied without hesitation. 'It's all different now. And I've lived in Sydney longer than I ever lived in Bombay. That's where my home is.' That is true. But despite my father's physical home being in Sydney, it has always been clear to me that it is India, not Australia, which has been the greater influence on his life, attitudes and values.

As we disembarked and collected our luggage, I noticed the three letters on my baggage tag: BOM. My brother informed me that even though this city's name is now Mumbai, the destination code has not changed. I too, had not really accepted this city's transition from Bombay to Mumbai. To me, this still felt like the Bombay of my parents' and grandparents' era. The city in my mind was some forty years younger than the modern day Mumbai which I was about to enter.

Our hotel was only about 25 kilometres from the airport, but the journey took us over an hour. Mumbai is notorious for its horrendous traffic, which is why one of India's most favoured forms of transport – the rickshaw – isn't allowed in the city centre. Even with the rickshaw ban, the traffic on that hot, winter afternoon was bumper to bumper. Alongside the seemingly endless stream of cars and taxis were people – hundreds, maybe even thousands of people. Everywhere I looked I saw Indian people, walking on the street, tapping on car windows begging for food and sitting on the pavement in clusters, homeless. I was mesmerised by the sheer number of human beings.

None of the stories I'd heard about Mumbai adequately prepared me for my first drive through the city streets. Admittedly, I had seen a few black-and-white photos of my father standing under some coconut palms with the ocean in the distance. But I certainly hadn't realised the architecture of the city was so influenced by the British. The streets surrounding our hotel, although jammed with cars and people, were quite well planned and the Gothic-style buildings rather beautiful.

I didn't have much time to admire the hotel surrounds, though. When we checked into our hotel, there was a message for my father from an old friend, requesting him to call her. We discovered she was going to arrive at our hotel in thirty minutes to take us to the home of one the few remaining Baghdadi Jews in Mumbai for *Shabbat* dinner.

Our host was a man by the name Freddy Sofer. Freddy is no longer alive, but he was renowned for his warm hospitality and for opening his home to Jews travelling through Mumbai, whether for business or on holiday, every Friday night.

Freddy's apartment was in the Mumbai suburb of Colaba. The remnants of Baghdadi Jewish life in Mumbai are centred in the Colaba district, rather than the Byculla area where the Benjamin family once lived. That is because there are many hotels, and therefore travellers, in Colaba. And although both the Sassoon-built synagogues are still standing, it is the Fort (Keneseth Eliyahoo) Synagogue which holds regular services.

It was dark by the time we arrived outside the entrance to Freddy's apartment building. From the outside, the building looked somewhat dilapidated. We climbed the two flights of stairs and were welcomed into Freddy's home. Other guests had already arrived, including a young French couple, an American businessman, an English lawyer, an Israeli man, Freddy's sister and a few women from the community. The French couple were invited for dinner after meeting Freddy in synagogue the previous week and the businessmen had been there before.

The apartment had a strangely familiar scent which it took me a moment to place. My father told me it was the smell of camphor. 'It smells like Nana's house,' I announced to him and my brother. They agreed. It looked a bit like her apartment too, as there were many photos of children and grandchildren in photo frames and on the walls. I instantly felt comfortable in this stranger's home. It was almost as if I had been there before. This feeling of being 'at home' is one I got surprisingly often while in Mumbai.

Freddy's apartment was actually one large room which had been subdivided into a living room, bedroom, dining room, kitchen and bathroom. The apartment was hardly luxurious. In fact, it was quite spartan. Yet, like the Benjamins decades before, Freddy had a cook who prepared dinner for us. Labour in India is so cheap that a cook is not considered a luxury.

Freddy's cook was an Indian woman who had been taught to prepare traditional Iraqi Jewish food. My father brought kosher wine all the way from Australia on which to make *kiddush* (the prayer over the wine), but Freddy was well stocked with Carmel-brand wine from Israel. My father led the prayers, singing the tunes which are so familiar to me and the other Baghdadi Jews, but clearly foreign to most of Freddy's guests. I realised how lucky I was to be able to make the trip to Mumbai with my father by my side.

The blessing on the *challah* (two braided loaves of bread made with egg) followed. In Sydney, *challah* is readily available at specialty kosher shops and even local supermarkets near my home. But I wondered who had made this *challah* as the demand for it in Bombay must be almost non-existent. I was told that the

71

challah was baked to order at the Taj Hotel. The Taj, made infamous during the 2008 Mumbai terrorist attacks, stands just in front of the Gateway of India landmark. It occurred to me that outside Israel, there is probably no other hotel in the world which bakes *challah* for its Jewish community.

My father told one of the Indian women that I sometimes bake *challah* at home. She was incredulous. 'You Western girls do everything,' she said to me. I laughed, reminding her that I do not have a cook to prepare my meals.

By the end of the night, I would happily have taken Freddy's cook home with me if she had agreed to come and, more to the point, if I could have afforded to pay her. Her food was delicious. The entire meal was meat-free and included salad with chickpeas, fried spicy vegetable patties served with coriander chutney, fish curry, rice, okra and vegetable *mahashas* (onion or cabbage rolls filled with rice and peas; the non-vegetarian version includes mince meat). It reminded me of my mother's tasty home cooking.

All of us were welcomed into Freddy's home as if we were his own family. We had more to eat than any of us could possibly have needed. This is the kind of warmth and hospitality that Indians – including the Jews of India – are known for. The kind of warmth and hospitality with which I grew up.

13. SHABBAT

The next morning was *Shabbat,* my first full day in Mumbai. I woke up to a view of the city skyline thick with smog.

Our hotel was situated on Marine Drive, a six-lane road which runs alongside Back Bay and past Mumbai's Chowpatty Beach. A wide promenade separates Marine Drive from Back Bay. Our hotel window faced the road, promenade and ocean, and I saw that on this weekend morning, there were women in saris and sneakers power-walking down the promenade. Some women walked alone, others were in groups. Their obvious wealth was in stark contrast to the impoverished Indians I'd seen sleeping on the street the previous night.

Aside from the sari-clad walkers, the promenade was filled with coconut sellers, bike riders and palm trees. It was a hive of activity. I knew it looked deceptively cool outside, when in reality, even at 8.00 a.m. it was already warm. Although Mumbai's average temperature is slightly cooler in the middle of the year, that is also monsoon time, which is why we chose to travel during India's winter.

Over breakfast, which was a mix of Indian and Western food, my father suddenly remarked, 'Who would have thought I'd ever stay in one of these fancy hotels in Bombay, when as a boy, I could only watch such people from afar?' As a boy living in a small apartment in Byculla with his many brothers and sisters, my father could only dream of hotels, buffet breakfasts and holidays.

After breakfast, we caught a taxi to the Keneseth Eliyahoo Synagogue for *Shabbat* morning prayers. The Synagogue was less than a five-minute taxi ride from our hotel. It is the same Synagogue in which my father's parents – Hannah and Jacob Benjamin – got married some eighty years ago.

I'd seen photographs of this Synagogue before, but the pictures I'd seen didn't capture the size of the building. It was much larger than I'd expected. The pale blue exterior of the Synagogue seemed almost out of place among the darker browns and greys of the buildings nearby. As I got closer, I saw that some of the blue paint was peeling off and the facade was in need of repair. Built in 1884, this Synagogue clearly showed its age. The problem is that the community for which this house of worship was built left Mumbai decades ago. Sadly, the few individuals that remain don't have the money required for maintaining the premises.

The Synagogue interior matched its pale blue and white exterior. Rather than individual seats, there were large wooden benches covered with cushions for congregants to sit on. In Orthodox Jewish synagogues men and women sit separately, and in this Synagogue the upstairs seating area would have been designated for the women. But on that Saturday there were hardly more than thirty people, so I sat with the handful of other women on one of the benches at the back of the Synagogue. The capacity of this Synagogue is around 300–400 people. I wondered how full it was on the day that Hannah and Jacob married here.

As I followed the prayers, I recognised the tunes as the same ones I have heard all my life in my family's Synagogue in Sydney. This must be one of the only synagogues in the world where I can hear the familiar prayer tunes of the Baghdadi Jews. I instantly felt comfortable, as if I had been here many times before, even though it was only my first visit. And for once, I didn't feel like an outsider in a synagogue other than Sydney's Sephardi Synagogue.

While I sat there, I observed the architecture of the building. Nothing was ornate, but there was a simple beauty about the room. There were rows of blue and white candy-striped columns supporting high white arches. Blue *Magen Davids* (Stars of David) surrounded by white circles were sitting in line with the top of each arch. Large stained-glass windows rested above the ark, which housed the Torah scrolls. Once the ark was open, I saw the Torah scrolls were encased in silver or teak and covered with colourful, sari-like material. Ceiling fans hung low and spun quietly. The fans were operated by non-Jewish attendants to circumvent the prohibition against using them on *Shabbat*. The air was refreshingly cool inside as we got a cross-breeze through the open windows, a welcome relief from the rising heat outside.

The exterior and interior of the Keneseth Eliyahoo Synagogue, 2003

Despite its tiny congregation, the Keneseth Eliyahoo Synagogue does hold regular services. As it so close to the hotel district, it is used by travellers to Mumbai. In fact, I noticed that many of the guests from Freddy's dinner the previous night were in synagogue that morning. The remnants of the Baghdadi community live in this area and also pray here.

Together with the other travellers, we were invited to stay for lunch after the service. It was only 11.30 a.m. and I was still full from breakfast, but I couldn't resist the traditional Iraqi food served. The meal was delicious. There was *zalata* (chopped tomato and cucumber salad), *potato bhaji* (spiced potatoes) and *hamim* (the traditional Sephardi *Shabbat* meal). As there are no kosher butchers in Mumbai anymore, the meat was slaughtered by a qualified *shochet* (a man authorised to kill animals in a manner which renders them kosher), most likely from the Bene Israel Jewish community. It was the only kosher meat we had during our entire four weeks in India.

Later that day, we walked around the streets of Colaba. Apart from the Synagogue, there was nothing to indicate that a Jewish community once existed and flourished in this area.

Despite the copious amounts of food we had already eaten that day, by the late afternoon I found my father discussing dinner plans with us. He suggested we go down to Chowpatty Beach for Indian snacks such as *bhel puri* (fried crisp wheat cakes), *chat patay* (boiled chickpeas and potatoes with spices), *paan* (betel leaf with pieces of betel nut, lime and spices, chewed regularly by many Indians), *kulfi* (Indian ice-cream), coconuts and fruit salad. The trip would be reminiscent of my father's boyhood, when he often went to the beach with friends on Saturday evenings after *Shabbat*.

We agreed to go down to Chowpatty Beach and found ourselves surrounded by Indian families and groups of friends. Only a handful of people were swimming in the ocean, but the sand was full of locals. There were Indian women in their colourful saris, children running around and playing games on the sand and extended families crowded on large rattan mats eating and drinking. The area was a synergy of bright colours, overpowering smells and loud chatter – a mix I experienced many times in India which I found an assault on my senses and to which I wasn't quite accustomed.

Next to the sand, there was a large concrete area filled with permanent food stalls. Most of the stalls were selling either *bhel puri* or *kulfi* and *falooda* (an Indian milk drink). One stand advertised itself as an 'ice and *gola* station' (*gola* is a slurpee compacted onto a stick). It sold snow cones and was lined with bottles of brightly coloured syrups with matching bottle tops – green, yellow, red, blue, orange and pink – to flavour the ice. The *bhel puri* stands had large plastic containers filled with *puri* fillings such as mung beans, tamarind paste, pepper water, diced tomato and, for *dahai puri*, yoghurt.

There were plastic bags full of pre-fried *puris* and metal bowls full of potato, onion and coriander. The stall holders were each vying for our business. 'What you want?' they called out in broken English, trying to entice us to buy their snacks.

As my father chose food from the array of stands, I could see he was positively beaming. He loved being back at Chowpatty. His previous visit to India had been with my mother and she wouldn't let him eat this 'street' food, fearing untreated water and poor hygiene. Clearly, this was not a fear he shared and he munched into *puris* and drank his pink *falooda* with delight.

The cost was miniscule and each of us fell into our beds that night exhausted and content.

14. BYCULLA

The following day was Sunday. We hired a taxi for the day to take us to Byculla, the suburb where the Benjamin family once lived. For eight hours or 80 kilometres, the cost was only 700 rupees, approximately 23 Australian dollars.

Byculla today is a predominantly Muslim neighbourhood and among the most impoverished parts of Mumbai. The travel guidebook I took with me to India described Byculla as follows:

> Byculla… epitomizes the grim legacy of nineteenth-century industrialization: idle chimney stacks, overcrowding and pavements strewn with ragged, sleeping bodies. The cotton-mills and sweat-shops are still here, churning out cheap clothes for the massive domestic market, but few can claim the turnovers they enjoyed a hundred years ago.[28]

There is no mention that this area was once a flourishing Jewish neighbourhood, complete with Jewish school, synagogue and *mikvah* (ritual bath); nor that Byculla was once a desirable area in which to live.

My father had never been back inside the apartment in which he grew up on Nagpada Road. On his previous visit, no one was home when he knocked on the door of his old apartment. This time we were hoping someone would be there to let us in.

Our taxi driver dropped us on Nagpada Road, right outside the entrance to the apartment building in which my father grew up. I was stunned by the filth and squalor surrounding us. The streets were dirty, with rubbish strewn alongside the pavement. The apartment building was run down on the outside, although my father commented that the interior courtyard was now in better condition than when he used to live there.

He grinned as he pointed out the stairs – which used to be wooden but are now concrete – where he and his brother Sammy used to throw water onto unsuspecting visitors and pick fruit from the baskets of preoccupied fruit vendors. We climbed the bare, dirty concrete staircase to the first floor and stood outside his apartment, which still had no number on its door or elsewhere to identify it. My father knocked. I was not expecting anyone to be home.

Within moments, however, a middle-aged man opened the door. He had dark skin and hair, but he did not look Indian. Speaking in Hindi, my father introduced himself and explained that he grew up in this apartment and asked if it would be possible for us to have a look inside. In true Indian style, we were welcomed into this stranger's home.

It turned out that two Muslim families were occupying my grandparents' old apartment. The configuration of the apartment, however, was very different from the days when the Benjamins lived there. The apartment had been subdivided and the man who answered the door, his wife and his father were living in one apartment, while his brother was living next door. The apartment we were inside comprised two rooms and a washroom. It was very small, but surprisingly clean and tidy. Quite a contrast to the street and exterior of the building.

To our mutual surprise, my father recognised the older gentleman. He was the same man who had bought the lease of the apartment from my father over thirty years earlier, when my father was leaving Bombay! After he bought the lease, he subdivided the apartment for his sons. We were amazed to discover that this family still had my grandparents' old wardrobe in their apartment, having bought it from my father at the time he sold them the lease.

It was difficult to imagine the Benjamins ever living here, because although they certainly did live in this apartment, the configuration was now significantly different. It seemed my father was a little disappointed to find the apartment in such an altered state, even though it had been thirty-five years since he'd left.

Despite our unannounced visit, this Muslim family were extremely hospitable to us. They offered us *chai* (tea), and within minutes, the younger man's wife had retrieved their wedding album and began showing us – complete strangers – their wedding photos, while my father chatted to the older man in Hindi. My father asked him about the other people who used to live in the building and was suddenly reminded of his former upstairs neighbour. While we were still looking at the wedding photos, my father went upstairs to meet this neighbour and soon came down and told us he wanted us to meet her.

I'd never heard my father, or any of my aunts and uncles, talk about their old neighbour Chingu. Yet when we were introduced to this Indian woman, Chingu, the never-heard-of-before upstairs neighbour, she treated us as if we were her own family. Chingu was wearing a beautiful pink sari. She calculated that she was eight years older than my father, but she didn't look it. Although her hair was greying, her skin was smooth and unwrinkled. And her eyes had a youthful twinkle to them.

Chingu told us that she was the youngest of her nine siblings; the same number of children as in my father's family. Chingu grew up alongside my father and his brothers and sisters in this building. But even after the Benjamins left for Australia, Chingu never married or had children of her own. Instead, she devoted her life to looking after her parents. They were no longer alive, but that is why Chingu never left the home in which she grew up.

Chingu was now retired, but she qualified and worked as a nurse for many years. She told us that she delivered my Aunty Margaret's three baby girls, my first cousins, at Bombay Nursing Home. She described my grandfather Jacob as 'a gentleman'. And she and my father reminisced about old times. They were both thrilled to see each other after over three decades apart.

Chingu's apartment, like the Muslim family's downstairs, was spotless. It was the exact size and layout of my father's old apartment, including the partitions separating the rooms. My father pointed out the intricate mosaic tiled floor in the living room, telling us that was exactly like the mosaic floor in his apartment which Nana used to scrub until it shone.

The apartment was a good size for Chingu, who now lived there alone. But it was almost impossible to believe that the eleven Benjamins and their aaya lived in a space this size. As much as I thought I would gain a better understanding of how my father lived in Bombay by being in this city, it was actually very difficult for me to visualise him ever living here. At least physically, it was extremely different from the home and life he has built for himself in Sydney.

We went onto Chingu's balcony. We were able to see the street below us, with its little squatter-type housing shacks erected by locals. As we looked across to the balconies and windows of other apartment blocks, my father pointed out to me where his Nani Habiba used to live. He showed me his best friend's apartment and the homes of other friends and extended family members. I now understand why the Benjamins had no need for a telephone – they would just yell out from their window and get the attention of whomever they wanted.

Chingu insisted that we stay for lunch. She phoned an order for food to be delivered to her apartment and ordered us to eat, yet she refused to eat herself. Chingu's sentences were peppered with the Hindi word *beta* which translates literally as 'son', but it is a general term of affection, similar to 'darling'. My brother, my husband and I were all Chingu's *beta*s. Her warmth and kindness were overwhelming. Her desire to have us all eat was one with which

I am familiar, her Indian hospitality reminiscent of the attitude of my extended family at home.

We reluctantly farewelled Chingu. My father promised to see her again before we were due to leave Mumbai.

Our next stop was the Magen David Synagogue in Byculla, the heart of the once-thriving Baghdadi Jewish community. This Synagogue is certainly off the tourist trail and, although many Jews who visit Mumbai stop in at the Keneseth Eliyahoo Synagogue in Colaba, it is generally those visitors whose families used to attend this Synagogue that come here. The Magen David Synagogue is the Synagogue that all members of my family – both the Benjamins and my mother's family – used to pray at when they lived in Bombay.

From the outside, the Synagogue looked to be in quite a dilapidated state. The pale yellow paint was badly peeling. Of the two *Magen Davids* which sat to the left and right of the 'Magen David Synagogue' lettering above the four columns at the building's entrance, the right star was so badly faded that it was barely visible. The massive clock tower was blackened in part. Clearly, this building was only a shadow of its former glory.

Inside, the Synagogue was empty, except for the constant stream of pigeons which flew in and out of the open windows. The ladies' gallery upstairs was covered in pigeon droppings and the brass plaques on which congregants' names had once been inscribed were no longer there.

It was extremely sad for me to see this unkempt house of worship, knowing that it had once been so treasured by my family and their community.

Yet my father was able to see past the decay and excitedly pointed out to me where he used to sit in this Synagogue and where his father and my maternal grandfather used to sit. He told me how on all the major Jewish festivals, this deserted building was filled to capacity. Now, it was simply a relic of times gone by.

The interior architecture of the Synagogue was not dissimilar to the Keneseth Eliyahoo Synagogue in Colaba. The ceiling looked about fifteen metres high and was supported by large pillars painted in yellow and white. Like in Colaba, there was no individual seating in the Synagogue. Rather, there were rows of wooden benches divided by small armrests. Wicker lined the base and back of the seats in between the wooden frames. The *teva* (elevated platform from which the reader conducts services, also known as a *bima*) was in the centre of the men's section and directly in front of it were the holy Torah scrolls. To access them, I had to walk up five steps and under an arch into a beautiful half-dome-shaped structure which was illuminated by countless lights. It was clear to me that this was once a very beautiful synagogue.

On my way out of this historic building, I noticed a small visitors' book and opened it to read the existing entries. As I scanned the pages, I saw that many of the visitors to the Synagogue had family members who sojourned in Bombay for a short time. Other families had been here for generations. Like me, they had come to see the city they had heard so much about; to see the Synagogue where their parents or grandparents married; to see the remnants of a community of which their relatives had been a part.

Some of the names in the visitor's book were familiar to me – names of people from Sydney's Sephardi community. Apart from Australians, entries in the book had been written by Israelis, Americans, Canadians and Britons. This Baghdadi community, which was so cohesive when it was centralised in Byculla, really has dispersed to all corners of the world.

After we left the Synagogue we walked to the Jacob Sassoon Free School. The school is literally next door to the Synagogue. This was the Jewish school which my father and his brothers and sisters attended. But now the only Jewish feature of the school was

The exterior and interior of the Magen David Synagogue, 2003

its name. Whereas the early lists of the school's honour students contained only Jewish names, the more recent entries were Indian-named students. I expect that not even in Jacob Sassoon's wildest imagination did he contemplate that the school he built for Baghdadi Jewish children would one day cater for a local Muslim population.

Behind the school building, we noticed about a dozen Indian boys involved in that ubiquitous activity we had witnessed all over the streets of India – a game of cricket. My father used to play cricket in that same area with his siblings and friends. After watching their game and briefly chatting to some of the boys about Australian cricketers, we piled back into our taxi for our last stop for the day: the Jewish cemetery – the cemetery in which my grandfather Jacob Benjamin is buried.

15. THE CEMETERY

Mumbai's Jewish cemetery is in the suburb of Chinchpokli, which is commonly referred to by the locals as Bakri Adda. It felt like the cemetery was in the middle of nowhere: it was approximately ten minutes by taxi from the centre of the Jewish neighbourhood in Byculla. Even once we arrived, there was little to indicate there was a burial ground in the area.

Admittedly, there was a simple white rectangular sign with black writing which stated 'Jewish Cemetery' outside the grounds. However, the sign was partially obscured by overgrown trees and was barely visible from inside the taxi. I'm not sure we would have found the cemetery at all if my father hadn't directed the taxi driver there.

The area adjacent to the cemetery was not unusual by Mumbai standards, but it really was quite a sight. The cemetery gates were surrounded by squatter-type housing. Identical shack-style structures had been erected across the street from the cemetery too. Above these shacks were squalid-looking apartment buildings, each balcony filled with colourful garments hanging out to dry on makeshift washing lines. Young boys played cricket on the street directly outside the cemetery. This is despite the fact that we were not on a suburban back street, but rather, on at least a four-lane road (give or take another lane; with the chaotic traffic and absent lane markings, it was hard to gauge exactly how many lanes of cars the Indians would manage here).

The gates to the cemetery were locked, but the caretaker opened them for us. Just inside the gates, a marble plaque read:

> Set apart forever by Elias David Sassoon Esq. in January 1878, as a Jewish burial ground in memory of his beloved son Joseph, who died at Shanghai in China on 22nd December 1868.

The cemetery was therefore established quite early in the history of the Baghdadi Jewish community. This is not unusual; one of the first things newly established Jewish communities do is to set up their own burial societies according to Jewish law.

It was exceptionally hot in the cemetery and not at all eerie. Other than the sound of trains going past in the background – there were train tracks just behind the cemetery – it was almost serene. And serenity is not something we found often in India, particularly Mumbai.

The cemetery was quite large, a useful indicator of the number of people who formed part of the Jewish community in preceding decades. Apart from a few frangipani trees, three mausoleum structures dominated the grounds. These massive structures were for three members of the Sassoon family: Sir Jacob Sassoon, his wife Lady Rachel Sassoon and his father Elias David Sassoon, each of whom had contributed so much to Jewish and secular life in Bombay.

The other graves were very close together and many of the inscriptions had worn away over time, which made it difficult to identify the deceased. My father, however, knew exactly where his father was buried.

The four of us – my father, my brother, my husband and I – were in tears before we were anywhere near my grandfather's grave. I was surprised by how emotional I felt, given this was a man I had never met. By the time we reached Jacob's grave, my father was openly sobbing. It was the first time in my entire life that I had seen him cry.

I felt quite overwhelmed to see my grandfather's tombstone.

This was the nearest I had ever come, and the closest I would ever get, to my grandfather. On that day, Jacob's life and ongoing presence became more real to me than they had ever been. Ironically, standing at my grandfather's grave and reading the inscription on his tombstone brought him to life for me; his death date and our tears were a tangible sign of the void created by his loss.

While we stood silently at Jacob's grave site, I knew my father was acutely aware that he had already lived a longer life than his own father. I silently prayed that I would have my father by my side for many, many, more years to come. As we turned to leave, each of us placed a stone on Jacob Benjamin's grave (it is Jewish custom to do so; stones represent permanence in contrast to the ephemeral nature of flowers).

My father led us through other parts of the cemetery, searching for the graves of other family members. He pointed out the graves of his two grandmothers, Nani Habiba and Nani Aziza. He also showed me the grave of one of my great-grandfathers, my great-great-grandfather (Jacob's grandfather, Chacham Avraham) and numerous great-uncles. It was obvious that this is where much of my family of generations past are buried. Whereas in the Jewish section of Sydney's cemeteries most of the dead have Ashkenazi names, here there were Mozelles and Levis and Sauls and Sassoons: familiar Iraqi names. And I felt a strange affinity to this place, something I have never felt in any cemetery before.

The majority of the graves were rectangular tombs with inscriptions on top of them. My grandfather's grave was in good condition as the Benjamin family had recently paid to have it repaired. Sadly, however, most of the other graves in this cemetery were in a state of complete disrepair. Many tombstones were cracked or broken and the inscriptions faded beyond recognition. My father explained that many of the graves had been plundered by poor locals, with gold being removed from the letters of the tombstones.

Nevertheless, my brother and I realised that we were extremely fortunate to be able to visit the graves of our relatives. Many Jews do not have this privilege, as their entire families were murdered in the Holocaust. All of my husband's great-grandparents were murdered by the Nazis, so they do not have grave sites anywhere in the world that he is able to visit.

From the inscriptions on the tombstones, a few things became clear to me. The first – evident from the death dates – was that the Baghdadi community lived in Bombay for little more than two generations. My own family were only in Bombay for one-and-a-half or two generations. The second was that, of the deceased, there was a mix of those born in Bombay and those born in Baghdad, with the majority born in Baghdad.

Ironically, even though the Sassoons were so wealthy and such integral sponsors of the Jewish community, their tombs were also in poor condition. There is simply no community here to regularly maintain the cemetery.

I left the cemetery with mixed emotions: distressed that so many of the graves were so neglected, yet also exceptionally fortunate to be able to visit the grave sites of so many of my relatives, especially my father's beloved father Jacob.

16. THE TIFFIN WALLAHS AND DHOBI GHAT

An account of my trip to Mumbai simply wouldn't be complete without describing the *tiffin wallahs* and the *dhobi ghat,* both of which were used by my mother's family while they lived in Bombay.

Like my father Abe, my mother Sheila was born and grew up in Bombay. Unlike the Benjamins, however, my mother and her siblings didn't attend the Jacob Sassoon Free Jewish School, so they missed out on being provided with free hot kosher lunches every day. However, Sheila and her sister still ate a hot kosher meal in the lunchroom of their all-girls Catholic school. And their father ate the same hot kosher lunch in his office in the city, as did their brother at his school. These lunches were prepared every morning by Sheila's mother Hilda and delivered to Hilda's husband and children via the unique and remarkable Bombay institution, the *tiffin wallah* or *daba wallah.*

A *tiffin,* or *daba,* is a cylindrical-shaped stainless steel or aluminium container. It is comprised of a number of individual round containers which stack on top of each other and clip together with a handle. Each individual container is filled with a different food, such as curry, rice or dhal. The tiffin wallah or daba wallah is the person who carries the tiffin and delivers it to its intended recipient.

Each weekday morning, my grandmother Hilda and her cook prepared lunch for the family. Some days it was samoosas; others it was curry and rice, or vegetables and rice, or a bhaji. The food was packed into the tiffin for delivery and was collected each morning from Hilda's apartment by the daba wallah. By the time Sheila and her sister arrived in their designated seats in their school lunchroom each day, the tiffins containing their home-cooked meals were there waiting for them. After they ate their lunch, the girls left the tiffins on the table to be collected by the daba wallah, who would deliver them back to Hilda at the apartment, ready for the next day's use.

Sheila's parents were far from wealthy. However, the daba wallahs were – and continue to be – so cheap that they are not at all a luxury for Mumbai's working or middle classes.

The success of the daba wallahs in delivering the correct lunch to the correct recipient is incredible. This is particularly so, given the scale of the operation (the daba wallahs deliver thousands of tiffins each day across Mumbai) and given that the tiffins have no name markings. Indeed, most of the daba wallahs are illiterate.

The impressiveness of the process is amplified by the fact that a bare tiffin is indistinguishable from another bare tiffin. The only way one tiffin is discernible from another is by a marking of coloured paint on the top, or by a bag in which the tiffin is sometimes placed by its owner. Further, it is not the same daba wallah who collects the tiffin each morning and then delivers it to the recipient. Rather, a series of daba wallahs operate to collect the tiffins, deliver them and then return them to their owners. Nevertheless, my mother declares that not once did she receive the wrong tiffin at school.

Our Mumbai travel guidebook informed us that at the time of its publication over ten years ago, around 4,000 daba wallahs delivered freshly cooked food from 125,000 suburban kitchens to offices in the downtown area.[29] It continued:

> Each lunch is prepared early in the morning by a devoted wife or mother while her husband or son is enduring the crush on the train … When the runner calls to collect it [the tiffin] in the morning, he uses a special colour code on the lid to tell him where the lunch has

to go. At the end of his round, he carries all the boxes to the nearest railway station and hands them over to other daba wallahs for the trip into town. Between leaving the wife and reaching its final destination, the tiffin box will pass through at least half a dozen different pairs of hands, carried on heads, shoulder-poles, bicycle handlebars and in … brightly decorated handcarts … Tins are rarely, if ever, lost, and always find their way home (before the husband returns from work) to be washed up for the next day's lunch.[30]

The guidebook also stated that, at the time it was written, most daba wallahs collected a measly one rupee (less than 4 Australian cents) for each tin they handled, creating an income of around 1000 rupees per month. The system creates a livelihood for poorer immigrants from the Pune area who operate it and provides a cheaper alternative to eating out for middle-income earners.[31] To catch the daba wallahs in action, the guidebook advised us to head for CST or Churchgate Railway Stations around late morning.

Intrigued, I was curious to see the daba wallahs in action while I was in India, so on our last day in Mumbai, my husband and I headed to Churchgate Railway Station. We arrived there at around 10.30 a.m. and took seats on the platform. Uncertain if were in the right place, we asked a few different passers-by where we might see the daba wallahs. None of them seemed to understand our question. It was as if we were speaking a foreign language. Although English is commonly spoken in Mumbai, we found many Indians had trouble understanding our Australian accents.

In this instance however, it didn't seem to be our accents that were causing the problem. Rather, it appeared to be the fact that we wanted to see the daba wallahs that was causing bewilderment. One Indian man misunderstood and thought we actually wanted to employ a daba wallah of our own, telling us that the daba wallahs must be hired on a monthly basis! He simply couldn't comprehend that we just wanted to watch the daba wallahs at work.

We noticed a man on the corner of the platform shining shoes. He looked like a regular, so we approached him, thinking he would know what time the daba wallahs usually arrived and where they tended to congregate. Despite the fact that this shoe-shine wallah was at Churchgate Station on a daily basis, he was surprisingly vague about the daba wallahs' activities. I soon realised that the daba wallahs are so much a part of everyday life in Mumbai, so exceptionally ordinary to the locals, that no one seemed to pay any attention to their coming and goings.

Finally, at 11.15 a.m. the tiffins began to arrive at Churchgate Station. Many of them were quite worn-looking, presumably from years of use. The procedure was very methodical and, as the tiffins arrived, they were sorted and redistributed for further delivery to their ultimate destination across town. I was surprised to observe that the movement of the tiffins wasn't particularly rapid. In true Indian style, the daba wallahs operated without any apparent sense of urgency.

Nevertheless, they were remarkable to witness. Many of the daba wallahs transported about twenty-five or thirty tiffins at a time, in large pallet-type structures which they carried above their heads. One of them crossed the road with a full pallet balanced above his head and proceeded to climb a hip-height concrete barrier which divided the road, while maintaining his load with just his left hand and his head.

I was incredulous and I have little doubt any Westerner would be. In Sydney's city where I have worked, it is hard enough as a pedestrian to dodge the always rushing bicycle couriers who deliver parcels and papers across town. In Mumbai, the daba wallahs were loaded with twenty-five lunch containers and had to work within the usual Mumbai traffic chaos of people, cars, taxis and road barriers everywhere. They did it with an ease, grace and almost serenity that I have never come close to seeing on any bicycle courier in Sydney.

The only thing which equalled my awe at the daba wallahs was my visit to Mumbai's central laundry, the *dhobi ghat*.

When my mother's family lived in Bombay, cheap labour meant they were able to afford not only daba wallahs, but also *dhobi wallahs* to do their laundry (*dhobi*). Every Sunday, the dhobi wallah came and collected the family's dirty laundry. The dhobi wallah then washed the clothes at the dhobi ghat, starched them, and returned them all ironed and properly folded. When the dhobi wallah returned the clothing, Hilda checked each article off against her list. My mother has commented that it is remarkable that hardly any items got lost in the process.

We were some of many tourists interested to see Mumbai's outdoor laundry and our taxi driver was not at all surprised when we asked him to stop at the bridge over the dhobi ghat so that we could take a photo. Our guidebook stated with authority that:

> This huge open-air laundry is the centre of one of those miraculous Indian institutions which, like the daba wallah's operation, is usually regarded by Westerners with disbelief. Each morning, washing from all over Mumbai is brought here to be thrown into soapy piles and thumped by the resident dhobi wallahs in the countless concrete tanks, barrels and shanty shacks inside the compound. The next day, after being aired, pressed, folded in newspaper and bound with cotton thread, the bundles are returned … The secret behind this smooth operation is a symbol marked on each item of clothing; each dhobi wallah has their own code – invisible to the untrained eye but understood by all in the washing business – that ensures the safe passage of laundry.[32]

The dhobi ghat was mind-boggling. Rows and rows of washing lines were filled with a rainbow of Indian attire. The whites and coloured items seemed to be separated. But among the coloured items there appeared to be no order or pattern: orange, green and pink *salwar kameez* (traditional Indian dress) hung side by side. Underneath the lines were rectangular troughs filled with pink, blue and green-tinged water. Some had clothes soaking in them, others were empty. Nearby, men and women were busy washing, wringing, hanging and sorting clothes. To me, it was difficult to comprehend that there was, and is, a precise order in this outdoor laundry which defies the outward appearance of chaos. Yet I knew that the dhobi ghat was just as reliable, if not more so, than any Western laundromat.

As a visitor to Mumbai, I am not sure how I could have had my clothes washed in the dhobi ghat even if I wanted to. But I realised that in the hot Mumbai weather, I desperately needed to do some laundry. My father's friend Lulu offered us the use of her 'servant'. Lulu told us to drop off our laundry at her apartment and she would arrange for our washing to be done. She suggested we leave a few hundred rupees as payment. We happily agreed, as the cost was significantly less than the price our hotel charged for laundry services.

Our laundry was washed at Lulu's apartment in a conventional washing machine, not at the dhobi ghat. Nevertheless, I found my clothes returned to me in better condition than when I wash them at home. Everything – including T-shirts and even underwear – had been starched, ironed and folded to perfection.

The institutions of the tiffin wallahs and the dhobi ghat are a window into the Indian mindset and way of life. As such, they helped me to understand how life in Bombay might have been for Nana Hannah and for my maternal grandmother Hilda. Seeing how the tiffin wallahs and the dhobi wallahs worked gave me just a glimmer of understanding as to why Hannah and Hilda had such a difficult time adjusting to life in the West once they left Bombay. In their new homes in Australia and the United States respectively, Hannah and Hilda had to do much of the housework which they had outsourced, or at least had help with, all their lives. It is no wonder it was a difficult transition for them both and that they had such fond memories of Bombay. Ironically, in spite of having whitegoods such as washing machines and refrigerators in their new homes, their Bombay lives were simpler and easier, and certainly more carefree.

I left Mumbai only five days after I arrived. Despite the brevity of my visit, spending time there allowed me to see the very foundations on which my life has been built. Being in Mumbai also gave me an understanding of many of the attitudes and values with which I was brought up and which have shaped me.

The other, more tangible, acquisition from my trip was a navy blue *challah* cover embellished with silver sequins. During one of my shopping expeditions in Mumbai, I unexpectedly stumbled upon a silk shop in the textile section of Crawford Market which specialised in Jewish materials. In addition to embroidered silk and velvet *challah* covers, the business custom made lavish *parochet* (curtains which sit in front of the Torah scrolls in a synagogue) for Jewish communities remaining in India and for an Israeli market. Surprisingly, they had been doing so for forty years.

I found it fitting that I was able to take home from the city of my ancestors an item of Judaica which I regularly use on my *Shabbat* table in Sydney. It is a constant reminder of my time in Mumbai, and of all the *challah* covers in my home, that one is my favourite.

PART 3

BOMBAY TO BONDI

17. FAREWELL BOMBAY: THE BENJAMINS

My departure from Mumbai wasn't a significant chapter in my life's history, but for my father Abe, my mother Sheila and their respective families, leaving India marked the end of an era. And the beginning of completely new lives.

Jacob Benjamin's death was not the precipitating factor for the Benjamin family's departure from India. Indeed, it was almost ten years after her husband Jacob died that Hannah left India. Rather, the Jewish community of which the Benjamins had been a part slowly began to disintegrate, which is what ultimately influenced the Benjamins to leave India.

Bombay's Jewish community started to crumble in the early 1950s. In 1951 there were 20,213 Jews living in Bombay, but by 1961 – only ten years later – this figure had decreased by almost 40 per cent to 12,366.[33] (Note these figures encompass not only Baghdadi Jews but also the Bene Israel and Cochin Jews.)

Two events led to the eventual collapse of the Baghdadi Jewish community in Bombay (and in other Indian cities, particularly Calcutta). The first occurred in 1947, with India gaining independence from Britain. The second occurred one year later in 1948, with the establishment of the State of Israel. The result was that Jewish emigration from India peaked in 1950–52.[34]

The wave of emigration following India's independence and the establishment of Israel had a snowball effect on the remaining Jewish community: as some families began to leave, marriage prospects for younger community members declined, and consequently, more and more Jews left India.

With the community dwindling, there was no future in Bombay for Hannah's children and grandchildren. Hannah's brother Hayeem and his family had already left Bombay for London in the early 1950s and Hannah's twin sister Sarah left for London in 1962. Hannah's brother Naji also eventually emigrated to London.

My father Abe didn't leave Bombay until 1966, but he refers to 1966 as the 'disintegration year' for his friends, as so many of them left Bombay that year for new homes in different countries. My mother Sheila and her family also left Bombay that same year.

It has been argued that the Baghdadi Jews were more motivated to leave India as a result of Indian independence rather than the creation of Israel.[35] Indeed, a number of historians emphasise the link between the Baghdadi Jews and the British, with Joan Roland going so far as to say that the Baghdadis seemed destined to leave once the British did and only those whose Zionism sufficiently out-weighed other opportunities went to Israel.[36] Orpa Slapak's view is that most Baghdadis didn't support Indian nationalism and didn't welcome Indian independence as they sought to identify with the British and distance themselves from the Indians.[37]

However, the reasons for the Baghdadi Jews leaving India en masse were manifold and cannot simply be attributed to India gaining independence from Britain. There were also economic reasons for the Baghdadi Jews' exodus from India: after 1947, new economic regulations enforced by the Indian Government restricted imports and controlled foreign exchange, which significantly affected the business of many wealthy Baghdadis. Further, the Arab boycott of the 1950s affected the Baghdadi Jews. Under this boycott, Arab countries and firms would not trade with any firms doing business with Israel, which made it very difficult for Baghdadi Jews to continue their trade with Arab countries, especially Egypt and Iraq.[38] Jews had to take in Indian partners and use Indian names.

In addition, some of the less affluent Baghdadis were affected by the closure of the Sassoon Mills in Bombay in 1945. In the 1930s, the Sassoons had transferred much of their business to China, but retained ownership of the Bombay mills. They closed the business in China at the start of World War II and shifted back to Bombay again. The final closure of the Bombay operations in 1945 resulted in many Jews losing their jobs and subsequently emigrating from India.[39]

Many Baghdadi Jews left India for the Commonwealth countries of Britain, Australia or Canada. Although Joan Roland states that only a small percentage of the Baghdadi community went to Israel and even less to the United States,[40] my father contends that most of the members of the Byculla community left India for Israel.

No member of the Benjamin family left Bombay during the so-called emigration peak of 1950–52. The first of the Benjamins to leave Bombay – Sass – didn't depart until 1960 and he went to London. Elaine left for Israel in 1961 with her husband and daughter. The rest of the Benjamin family emigrated to Sydney, Australia.

Florrie, the eldest of the siblings, was the first to leave Bombay for Sydney. She arrived in Sydney in 1962 with her husband and two daughters. Margaret and her family followed in 1964, together with her youngest sister Mabel. The eldest of the Benjamin brothers, Benny, sailed from Bombay in late 1965. His wife, two children and brother Sammy followed early in 1966. After that, only Hannah, her youngest child Isaac and my father Abe remained in Bombay.

The years following Jacob's death had not been easy for Hannah. Yet she was very reluctant to leave India, the only home she had ever known. In late 1965, Hannah's immigration papers came through, which plunged her into a state of depression. She was terrified of leaving India; terrified at the prospect of leaving everything that was familiar to her, moving to a new country and starting a new life.

Concerned about their mother's mental health, Hannah's children kept her on tranquilisers for the three months prior to her departure from Bombay. All of the other family members had travelled to Sydney by ship, but in her depressed state, Hannah would not be able to endure the long sea voyage. Her children realised they needed to get the fifty-three-year-old matriarch of the family to Sydney as soon as possible – which meant by air. They therefore used a large proportion of the little money they had to buy two airline tickets: one for Hannah and one for their youngest brother, Isaac. In March 1966, Hannah and twelve-year-old Isaac travelled on an Air India flight from Bombay to Sydney.

With Hannah and Isaac gone, Abe was now the only one of the Benjamins left in Bombay. He had resigned from his job and taken all the leave he had accrued in order to sell the family's belongings and pack up their home. Even though the Benjamins leased rather than owned their apartment, Abe was able to sell the lease because people were willing to pay money to take over existing tenancies due to a housing shortage.

Abe negotiated the sale of the Benjamins' tenancy with their landlord and his lawyer on the basis that the Benjamins paid the landlord a percentage of the money received for transferring the lease. Abe sold the lease to a young Muslim man – the same man who was living in the Benjamins' old apartment during our visit to Mumbai in 2003. The sale of the lease provided finance for Hannah, Abe, Sammy and Isaac's passage to Australia.

With the lease sold, Abe had to vacate the apartment. He moved in with his uncle, Hannah's brother Naji, and waited for his immigration papers to arrive. Abe had applied to immigrate to Australia the previous year, 1965, but it wasn't until his sister

Florrie applied from Australia to sponsor him that Abe's papers came through. After passing his medical examination and receiving a police clearance, Abe obtained his visa and booked his ticket to Australia.

My father was not sad to leave India. Rather, he was quite anxious to get out as most of his friends had already left or would be leaving soon. He was especially looking forward to being reunited with his mother and most of his brothers and sisters, some of whom he had not seen for four years as they had left India long before him.

Abe travelled to Australia on an Indian passport. As an Indian citizen emigrating to a foreign country, he wasn't allowed to take money out of India with him. When Abe left Bombay, he was only permitted to take 40 rupees – equivalent at that time to A\$7 – with him.

It wasn't as though Abe had a great deal of money anyway. When he sold the lease on the family's apartment, he did so for 45,000 rupees, equivalent to approximately A\$7,000. Of that amount, the landlord took about 12,000 rupees, roughly one quarter of the total. Part of the remaining money was used to repay Hannah's brother Naji, who had loaned money to Hannah in order for her to have clothes made for herself and her children prior to leaving for Australia.

This left only a few thousand Australian dollars. That money was transferred to Sydney via London using Bombay agents of a London firm. As this transfer of funds was illegal, the family was forced to pay double the exchange rate. The result was that they lost half of their already meagre savings. With so little money, it was imperative for each of the Benjamins to find work as soon as they arrived in Sydney.

My father was twenty-two years old when he sailed for Sydney on 15 May 1966 on the P&O liner *Oronsay*. It was the first time he had ever been out of India.

The sea voyage from Bombay to Sydney took fifteen days. Although not planned in advance, Abe ended up sailing with a Bombay friend, Reuben Shellim. Reuben was to be best man at Abe's wedding in Sydney some four years later.

With only A$7 each in their pockets, Abe and Reuben referred to themselves as 'the penniless passengers'. They got the cheapest cabin they possibly could, which was at the very bottom of the ship. Abe and Reuben shared a four-berth cabin with two other men, including an Indian man who was travelling back to his New Zealand home. Abe cannot remember this man's name, but he does remember he had a box of mangoes and was constantly giving Abe and Reuben mangoes to eat.

I am not surprised that my father, long ago nicknamed 'Fruits Benjamin' by one of my uncles, remembers the free mangoes. One of my father's great delights is to buy mangoes by the caseload when they are in season, regardless of which country he is in. Even when we were holidaying in Mumbai months before the beginning of the peak mango season, the table in my father's hotel room was covered with mangoes.

The trip to Sydney was a great experience for Abe as he'd always wanted to go on a sea voyage. In fact, he's loved cruises ever since. However, having so little money was quite constraining for the two young men. The cost of Abe's ticket to Sydney included meals and entertainment, but nothing else. They could only watch while the other passengers bought drinks and duty-free goods and went on shore excursions. Abe and Reuben generally kept to themselves and didn't socialise much with the other passengers. Abe did play a few games of bingo on board and occasionally won a few shillings (the *Oronsay* was an English ship and therefore English currency was used) but the few shillings prize money didn't buy much.

En route to Sydney, the *Oronsay* stopped briefly in Colombo, Fremantle, Adelaide and Melbourne. Abe finally arrived in Sydney on 30 May 1966. He was standing on one of the decks of the ship as the *Oronsay* docked at Wharf Number 13 Pyrmont, when he caught sight of his sisters Florrie and Margaret waiting to greet him. Abe was thrilled to see them. He was particularly excited to be reunited with Florrie, whom he was very close to and hadn't seen in over four years.

Abe was taken by taxi to his new home, which was actually a house subdivided into two tenancies: 1/54 Brighton Boulevard, Bondi. He was to live there for the next three and a half years with his mother and younger siblings Mabel, Sammy and Isaac. His elder siblings Florrie, Margaret and Benny lived in their own homes with their respective families, but none of them were far away. In fact, all the Benjamins residing in Sydney lived in the heart of Sydney's Jewish community in the suburb of Bondi, within walking distance of each other. The only two missing were Sass in London and Elaine in Israel. And of course, their father, Jacob.

18. SYDNEY, AUSTRALIA

My father has always loved photography. He took countless photos of the Benjamin family's early years in Sydney: photos of Hannah's children and grandchildren playing cricket together, eating together, swimming, sunbaking and generally enjoying Australian life. They look really happy.

But the photos are deceptive. They make it look as though the Benjamins and their spouses and children lived easy, uncomplicated lives. In truth, each of the Benjamins had to work hard and most struggled financially in their early years in Sydney. Although some of them made the transition to Australian life smoothly, for others that transition wasn't as effortless as the photos make it seem.

Hannah in particular found life in Sydney challenging. Having not wanted to leave Bombay, she was at first extremely unhappy in Sydney. She had lived all her fifty-three years in India and now she felt isolated, restricted and lonely in her Bondi home. Faced with a foreign culture and a new way of life, Hannah was anxious and depressed. She had none of the domestic help and companionship of neighbours to which she was accustomed.

Hannah desperately wanted to return to Bombay and kept threatening to take her youngest son, Isaac, and go back there. 'I was bored [in Sydney],' she told me; 'I used to cry and cry, "Send me back to Bombay".' It was only when her son Sass emigrated from London to Sydney in 1967 via the ten-pound scheme (whereby British subjects were offered their fare to Australia for only ten pounds per person) and offered to buy her ticket back to Bombay that Hannah realised there was nothing left for her there. After that, she began to accept Sydney as her new home. Her depression lifted and eventually she became extremely independent and self-sufficient, in the way I always remember her being.

Interestingly, Hannah's twin sister Sarah similarly didn't like London at first after all her years in Bombay. Sarah recalls her first London winter being so bad that she too wanted to return to Bombay. But Sarah, like Hannah, eventually adapted to her new life in a new city.

In comparison, my father Abe was fortunate in that he adapted quite easily to Sydney life. Doubtless, Abe's adjustment was also eased by the fact that he was young and that he moved into an established family home and Sephardi Jewish community.

In addition, Abe didn't find it difficult to secure a job; he arrived as an immigrant so had permanent residency status and was entitled to unemployment benefits while he searched for work. It only took him a few weeks to find a job. He had finished his trade qualifications in Bombay as an air-conditioning serviceman at Voltas Ltd and he got a job repairing refrigerators at a whitegoods firm named Simpson Pope in Sydney.

However, life in Sydney was by no means easy for Abe. The Benjamin family had little money and those of Hannah's children living with her – Abe, Mabel and Sammy – each had to bring in an income to support both their mother who didn't work and was too young to receive a government pension, and their youngest brother Isaac who was still at school. Abe was responsible for paying the rent while Sammy and Mabel's incomes were utilised for payment of food, utilities and other outgoings.

At that time, Abe says, his life was all work. He spent three hours each day commuting to and from work on public transport and had to leave home before 6.30 a.m. each morning. His salary was the very modest sum of $46 per week. Half of that was dedicated to paying the $23 per week rent on the Brighton Boulevard house. Most of the balance was put towards expenses, including travel, although he did manage to save $10 each week. To earn extra money, Abe tried to get additional work wherever possible, such as doing some cleaning at the nearby grocery store, Eze & Son.

Abe has never forgotten that time in his life. When my brother and I were children, our father often told us how difficult it was for him in his early years in Sydney. He was not complaining, but rather, hoping he would inspire us to study hard so that we would never be in a similar situation and have to engage in physical labour. My brother and I heard the same stories so many times that we used to joke that 'when Dad first arrived in Australia he used to walk ten miles in the snow just to save five cents' – even though it never snowed in Sydney and we've been on the metric system for decades. Needless to say, our father wasn't particularly amused.

It was only years later that I began to realise how tough it had been for my father and why he continues to be so financially conservative. And why he worked so hard to provide us with a good education – so we would have choices and opportunities which were never available to him.

Although they had little money, there was still a simplicity about the Benjamins' lifestyle at the time that I find myself envying. The family, so close in Bombay, remained so in Sydney. They continued to socialise with each other, and family life and Judaism were of paramount importance. Physically and emotionally, they were very close.

During the week, the siblings were busy at their respective jobs or with their children so they didn't see much of each other, but they did spend occasional weekday evenings watching television together. TV was one of the perks of Sydney life that the Benjamins could only have dreamed of in Bombay. Granted, Hannah and her younger children couldn't afford a TV to begin with. But six months after my father arrived in Sydney, they bought a black-and-white TV via hire purchase for their Brighton Boulevard home. And before that, they could go over to Florrie or Margaret's homes to watch TV there. Still, colour television was a luxury that wasn't introduced into Australia until years later in 1975.

It was on the weekend that the Benjamins really spent a lot of time together. Sunday mornings were generally reserved for housework, but in summer the Benjamins spent many Sunday afternoons swimming at nearby Bondi Beach. And every Saturday, beginning in the late afternoon, Hannah's Brighton Boulevard home where Abe, Mabel, Sammy and Isaac lived became the meeting place for the other brothers and sisters (Florrie, Benny and Margaret) and their families. Hannah cooked traditional Iraqi food such as *aloomakalas*, *chittarnee* and *hamim*. The Benjamins socialised, ate and played cards together. In summer, the males and the kids played cricket in the front yard of their home and on the street and the women sat and talked.

Abe Benjamin, Brighton Boulevard, Bondi, 1968

Hannah Benjamin, Sydney, 1969

Even when all Hannah's children had moved out of her home and into homes of their own, they continued to meet each Saturday evening at her place. This tradition continued even when the younger grandchildren such as my brother and I were born. At about eight years old, I distinctly remember wondering what my cousins and I would all do on Saturday nights if Nana suddenly died. Obviously, Nana was never going to live forever, but I needn't have worried. Our weekly Saturday visits to Nana's house stopped years before her death.

Sydney's Jewish Community

Although he spent a lot of time with his family, my father also became involved in the Sydney branch of his Bombay Jewish youth group, Bnei Akiva, or 'BA', as it was commonly known.

BA organised many activities for Jewish youth in Sydney which Abe, his brother Sammy and his sister Mabel sometimes attended. In this way, they met their Ashkenazi Jewish contemporaries in Sydney. However, unlike many of the other young Jewish men and women who went to BA functions, Abe, Sammy and Mabel were not studying at university but were working. This meant they could only participate in BA's weekend activities and could never go away to camp, as they had done in Bombay. Nevertheless, Abe's transition into Sydney life was certainly eased by his affiliation, albeit limited, with BA.

Abe's primary affiliation with the Jewish community in Sydney was not, however, with Bnei Akiva but with Sydney's Sephardi Synagogue. Abe made new friends through the Sephardi Synagogue, some of whom he still counts as his closest friends even though they no longer affiliate with the Synagogue.

When Abe arrived in Sydney, he was welcomed into the Sephardi community and offered membership at half the usual cost, as he couldn't afford full membership fees. He accepted the offer and became very involved with the Synagogue, which at that time was the only Sephardi synagogue in Australia. Abe was fortunate to arrive into this established Sephardi community which followed his own customs and traditions. His adjustment to life in Sydney was made much easier than it may otherwise have been, as he was able to meet and socialise with his 'own' people who followed the same customs.

Sydney's Sephardi Synagogue has a special place in my heart. It has been part of my life for as long as I can remember. I feel at home there in a way I haven't felt in any other synagogue in the world – except perhaps the Fort Synagogue in Mumbai. I have spent hours and hours there, praying, playing, eating and contemplating life. It is the Synagogue in which my parents married, in which I spent most of my childhood *Shabbat* mornings, in which I married, and in which my son had his *brit milah* (circumcision).

Sydney's Sephardi Synagogue was built in 1962, so by the time my father Abe arrived in 1966 it was reasonably well established. Located in Bondi Junction, it was only five minutes by car from Abe's Brighton Boulevard home, although it was a solid 45 minutes by foot – a much longer walk than the Magen David Synagogue which was only two minutes away from Abe's childhood home in Bombay.

The founding members of the Sephardi Synagogue, the Aarons, had emigrated to Sydney from Calcutta, India. Funds to establish the Synagogue were provided by benefactor Jacob Aaron, London's Spanish and Portuguese congregation and the World Sephardi Federation.[41] When the Synagogue was first established it did not have its own rabbi and so adopted the Sephardi Chief Rabbi of London as its spiritual head. By the time Abe arrived in Sydney in 1966, a rabbi had been appointed – Rabbi Simon Silas – and the Synagogue had a Board of Management.

Rabbi Silas was the first ever Sephardi rabbi in the Southern Hemisphere. Born in Calcutta, India and trained in Israel and Manchester, he was twenty-six years old when he arrived in Sydney from London in August 1963. He arrived in a community that did not hold services on a daily basis. Regular services were only held on Friday evenings and Saturdays. (Indeed, when Rabbi Silas left Sydney in 1980, the community still did not hold regular weekday services.) Rabbi Silas represented the Sephardi community in the wider Sydney Jewish community. He was an Orthodox rabbi who was well suited to the congregation, and he was both liked and respected. He was also the rabbi who would marry my parents in 1971.

The fledgling Sephardi community faced numerous challenges. One was that of meeting the needs of its Sephardi constituents who originated from different countries and had varying traditions.

When Abe arrived in mid-1966, the majority of Sydney's Sephardi community originated from India, Singapore and Egypt. However, the community also consisted of Jews from Burma, Shanghai and Lebanon. These varying countries of origin meant there were many different customs and traditions within the community which had to be reconciled. While Rabbi Silas was the presiding minister, the congregation followed the Spanish and Portuguese traditions. In the post-Silas years, the Synagogue's Religious Committee tried to standardise the services, including the prayer books, and as the community grew it moved more to the Iraqi style and used Iraqi prayer books.

Another challenge faced by the Sephardim was to establish themselves as equal yet distinct members of Sydney's wider Jewish community, which was and is a predominantly Ashkenazi community. The Baghdadi Jews of India who had emigrated to Sydney were in the unfamiliar situation of being a minority within the Jewish community, rather than part of the majority.

Rabbi Silas battled to have Sephardi rights and customs recognised within Sydney's Jewish community. He eventually became a member of the NSW Kashrut Board and the Beth Din (Jewish rabbinical court), but even this was a struggle as the Beth

Din opposed his admission, arguing they had enough members. The Sephardi community argued back that they were a separate entity and needed their own representation. Eventually, Rabbi Silas became a *dayan* of the Beth Din (a judge on religious and marital disputes between members of the community) and also represented Sephardi matters before the Beth Din.

The entire Benjamin family became integral members of the nascent congregation and worked to raise funds and help build up the community. The family was very community oriented and the Benjamins were always willing to volunteer their time and energy. They helped organise and run fetes at the Synagogue to raise money and did whatever they could to assist, even if it was as simple a task as moving furniture.

Hannah, her daughters and daughters-in-law helped other members of the Ladies Auxilliary prepare traditional Iraqi food for the Synagogue fetes such as vegetable *samoosas*, *chat patay* and *bhajias*. Despite being such an accomplished cook, Hannah was always eager to learn new recipes and she learnt from some of the other Sephardi women how to bake cakes – different from the ones she baked in India, like pineapple upside-down cake – and would then go home and replicate the recipes.

Abe, a proficient Hebrew reader, was asked to conduct synagogue services, including reading from the Torah. Towards the end of 1969, Abe was elected onto the Board of Management as Councillor and in following years held positions of Councillor, Assistant Secretary and Secretary.

The Benjamin family became one of the four largest families in Sydney's Sephardi community. Three of Hannah's children married within four months of each other, all at the Sephardi Synagogue. One of those was my father Abe, who married my mother Sheila in April 1971.

19. THE JACOB FAMILY

My parents, Abe and Sheila, were both born in Bombay. Sheila, however, was born in October 1948 – almost five years after Abe. Although they both grew up in the same Byculla Jewish community, Sheila's childhood was considerably different from Abe's.

In the Benjamin household, Hannah was the undisputed 'boss'. In contrast, it was Sheila's father Ezekiel (known as Eze) who was dominant in her family's home. He was particularly strict and exacting with his three children.

Eze Jacob, my maternal grandfather, was born in Rangoon, Burma (now Myanmar) on 1 August 1914. Eze's father Fred was similarly born in Rangoon in 1890; his mother Mozelle was born in Iraq in 1896. Like my paternal great-grandmother Aziza, my great-grandmother Mozelle was only a girl when she married – she was fifteen years old. Mozelle and Fred had five children together, all born in Rangoon: Mordechai (Mordy), Eze, Emily, Thelma and Solomon.

Mozelle was a kind and gentle woman who taught her children to appreciate the little things in life that she told them God had given them. She and Fred were religious Jews and all five of their children attended a Jewish school in Rangoon. Their second son, Eze, was transferred at age fourteen from his Jewish school to an English high school, where he was educated for a further two years.

However, in 1930, when Eze was only sixteen years old, his father died from a snake bite. Eze's father Fred was only forty at the time and Fred's premature death had enormous repercussions. Eze had to leave school in order to financially support his mother and two younger sisters and brother, who were then aged thirteen, ten and four respectively. Even though Eze was not the eldest male in the family, he assumed the role of breadwinner for his mother and younger siblings – an enormous responsibility for such a young man.

Eze took up a job in a photographic studio where he worked six days a week (excluding Saturday, *Shabbat*), from 9.00 in the morning to 9.00 at night. The twelve-hour days continued for seven years, during which time Eze had not a single holiday. These formative years of relentless work and financial responsibility meant Eze had to be exceptionally diligent, without any time for fun or pleasure. Unsurprisingly, this shaped Eze's attitudes and expectations when he raised his own children many years later.

Fred's death was also very difficult for his wife Mozelle, who was only thirty-five years old when she was widowed. Eze's sister Thelma remembers their mother sewing dresses late at night with a hand machine in order to get some money for the family.

In late 1941 during the World War II, Eze, his mother and siblings escaped Rangoon via sea on the SS *Chilka*. They got out of Burma just in time, as the Japanese bombed Burma in March 1942. The *Chilka* sailed to Calcutta, where the Jacob family briefly sought refuge, after which they continued to Bombay where they eventually settled. Other Burmese Jews similarly left Burma for India during the war, some of them even travelling by foot through the mountains between Burma and East India.

Of his mother and four siblings, it would be Eze who would remain in Bombay the longest.

Hilda Levy, my maternal grandmother, was born in Bombay in May 1922. In comparison to Eze, Hilda's childhood was happy and carefree. She was the youngest of seven children and was doted on by her adoring four brothers and two sisters. By her own admission, her siblings 'pampered her too much'. With just a hint of wistfulness in her voice, Hilda used to say that she lived like a princess in her mother's home.

Hilda's mother Rachel was born in Bombay in 1881 and her father Abraham was born in Aden. Rachel's youngest daughter Hilda was very similar in character to her mother: kind, gentle, caring and giving.

The Levy family was a very musical one. Of the two rooms which comprised their Bombay apartment, one stored all the children's musical instruments, including a piano, violin and harmonium (a reed organ). Hilda played the piano and loved to sing and go dancing with her brothers Isaac, a professional dancer, and Joe.

In fact, Hilda adored all her brothers and her father Abraham. Abraham loved to spoil his children, especially when they were sick, treating them to chocolates and imported Jacob's Cream Crackers from England.

Hilda enjoyed school and, like most of the other Baghdadi Jewish children, she attended the Sir Jacob Sassoon Free School. It was only a five-minute walk from her home in Byculla's Jumma Sheriff Building. Hilda's life as a young girl in her parents' home was extremely happy.

In later years, Hilda's brother Joe became friendly with Eze Jacob. Both Eze and Joe were observant Jews and used to meet each other at Bombay's Byculla Synagogue. Eze, Joe discovered, had arrived in Bombay from Rangoon with his mother and siblings.

It was from their frequent meetings that Joe formed the opinion that Eze would be a good match for his youngest sister Hilda; Eze was religious, responsible and came from a good family. Joe liked Eze very much and told Hilda that Eze was the right man for her and that she should marry him. And so, when Hilda was twenty-three years old, Joe arranged her marriage to Eze Jacob.

Hilda loved and greatly respected her brother Joe. So even though another man was in love with Hilda and constantly pursued her, she did not marry him. Joe's opinion of this suitor was that he was lazy and irresponsible as he was constantly changing jobs, and that he would not make a good husband for Hilda.

Decades later, Hilda told me that she didn't wish that she married this other man. However, she readily admitted that she had no choice in the matter of who she married. After explaining to me the arrangement Joe made between her and Eze, she told me plaintively: 'I got married to him' [Eze].

I was stunned by the matter-of-fact manner in which my grandmother Hilda made this statement. It was as if she had told me what she'd had for lunch that day, not about an event which was to change her life dramatically. Her mind-set was best expressed by the rhetorical question which both she and Nana Hannah often posed: 'What to do?' The Baghdadi Jewish women of my grandmothers' generation resigned themselves to their lot in life without much fuss. Thankfully, their reluctance to challenge the status quo is an attitude which no longer prevails.

I can see that Joe was acting in what he considered to be his sister's best interests and that his primary concern would most likely have been the ability of a prospective husband to financially support his sister and their future children. But with the benefit of hindsight, it seems to me that Joe's choice was not the best one for Hilda.

Hilda and Eze married on 5 September 1945, only three or four months after Joe recommended they marry. Hilda was twenty-three years old, Eze thirty-one. Their wedding was held in Byculla's Magen David Synagogue and the reception at the Cowasjee Jehangeer Hall in the Fort area of Bombay. I'm not sure why, but not a single photograph was taken of their wedding.

Amazingly, my paternal grandfather, Jacob Benjamin (who was a friend of Eze's brother Mordy), was a witness at Hilda and Eze's wedding! Neither of my parents were aware of Jacob's presence at Hilda and Eze's wedding – let alone his role as witness to their marriage – until some twenty-five years later when they had to produce Hilda and Eze's *ketubah* (marriage certificate) prior to their own wedding. It's strange that neither Hilda nor Eze thought to mention this to my mother because it seems so significant to me.

My grandfather Jacob could never have been at my own parents' wedding as he died years earlier. But it does seem like a good omen that he witnessed my mother's parents' wedding. Maybe I'm making too much of it, but it's as if in some small way Jacob Benjamin gave his blessing to my parents' marriage by witnessing Eze and Hilda's.

Once married, Hilda and Eze lived among Bombay's Baghdadi Jews in Byculla, not far from the Benjamin family. Hilda and Eze only had three children – a small family by the standards prevalent in their community at the time. Their eldest daughter Sheila (my mother) was named after Eze's maternal grandmother; their other two children, Mozelle and Fred, born in 1951 and 1957 respectively, were named after Eze's mother and father.

However, Hilda and Eze's marriage, although it produced three children and lasted a lifetime, was not a happy one.

Eze was a good provider for his family. But Hilda and Eze simply weren't suited to each other. They argued a lot; Eze had a very bad temper and Hilda's way of coping with his anger was simply to ignore him. Eze got annoyed with Hilda because she wouldn't listen and this cycle of poor communication continued.

Decades later, Hilda told me that she had wanted to divorce Eze in the early years of their marriage, but her family wouldn't let her. A divorce would have caused her family much shame. Hilda says that she wishes she had divorced Eze, but acknowledged that by the time she admitted that to me, it was much too late. She says he always wanted to have things his way, something she didn't know about him until after they were married. I asked her if she was ever happy with her husband and, almost too embarrassed to admit it, she quietly replied, 'no'.

Eze did actually threaten Hilda with divorce a number of times (he found her infuriating too), but this was after they had children and left India, by which time Hilda would never have remarried and it would have been completely impractical for her to live as a divorced woman. I feel immense sadness for both my grandparents in that they endured their marriage rather than enjoyed it. How blessed we are to live in an era and a country where we are free to choose our own partners and where divorce, although not desirable, is not a stigma but an acceptable and viable option to escape an unhappy marriage. If only it could have been that way for Hilda and Eze:

20. FATHER KNOWS BEST

Hilda and Eze Jacob and their three children lived in an apartment in the same building in which Hilda grew up: the Jumma Sherriff Building on 2nd Peerkhan Street, Byculla, Bombay. Almost the whole building was occupied by Jewish tenants. The Jacobs' living conditions were not dissimilar to the Benjamins', save for the fact that they simply had fewer people living in one home as their family was smaller.

The Jacobs' apartment was very basic and had only two rooms. One room was the kitchen where all the cooking was done and all the food products were stored. There was a stove and a gas cylinder with cooktop, but no oven. Like the Benjamins, the Jacobs had no running water. Their kitchen therefore housed big drums which were filled with water by the aaya each morning, and a large earthenware pot where water was stored for drinking after it was boiled. The earthenware helped to keep the water cool in the Bombay heat. Like the Benjamins, the Jacobs didn't have a refrigerator, but there was an icebox in which they were able to chill perishable items.

The other room in the apartment was simply a large room which the family used as a dining room during the day and where all five family members slept each night. The floor in this room was covered with colourful mosaic tiles, just like the mosaic floor I saw in Chingu's apartment while visiting Mumbai. Sheila, Mozelle and Fred did their homework at the dining table in this room, and Eze did his work there. Unlike the Benjamins, each family member had a proper bed and no one slept on mattresses on the floor.

The Jacob family shared only three outside bathrooms with the residents of seventeen other apartments. Despite Eze's efforts in liaising with the municipality and organising cleaners to help keep the building clean, the standard of hygiene was very low, which caused a lot of illness.

Dysentery, diarrhoea and diphtheria were rife in Bombay, as were smallpox and cholera, although vaccinations were available to prevent the latter two diseases. Sheila and Mozelle, for example, received compulsory vaccinations at school for smallpox and cholera. Both the girls managed to escape any serious childhood illnesses but their brother Fred got diphtheria when he was four years old. Such were the challenges of living in Bombay.

One of the plusses of living in Bombay was the companionship and support provided by Hilda's extended family. Hilda's family, to whom she was very close, lived near the Jacob family. After Hilda's father Abraham died, Hilda's mother Rachel moved in with her eldest daughter Nancy. Nancy lived less than a ten-minute walk away from Hilda and Eze's home. Hilda's brother Joe and his family were even closer – they lived next door to Hilda and Eze. Later, when Joe moved out, Hilda's other brother Sayeed moved into the next-door apartment.

Hilda used to visit her mother Rachel four or five times a week, often taking her children with her. My mother Sheila recalls that she regularly went to visit her Nani Rachel, sometimes on Saturday afternoons where she ate the traditional Sephardi *Shabbat* lunch of *hamim*.

Like my paternal grandmother Hannah, my maternal grand-mother Hilda had a lot of help at home in Bombay. She had a live-in aaya who was considered part of the Jacob family and she also had a cook named Mistry. Mistry didn't live with the Jacob family but came to their apartment every morning in time to collect the water to fill the water tanks. After that, Hilda and Mistry planned the menu for the day's meals before Mistry went on his daily trip to the market to buy fresh food.

Mistry bought kosher meat, fish and vegetables as required by the menu, and then prepared the meal under Hilda's supervision. And if he bought more than he could carry, Mistry would get a *pati wallah* to walk with him. The pati wallah was essentially a home delivery service, balancing a basket on his head filled with all the items a shopper had bought but was unable to carry. Unsurprisingly, the cost of engaging a pati wallah was negligible.

Like most of the other Baghdadi Jewish women of her generation, Hilda didn't work outside the home. Eze, in contrast, was always juggling a few different jobs. After he arrived in Bombay, Eze took a shorthand and typing course. He first worked as a secretary and then a stenographer, and kept working as a stenographer until he left Bombay. He also took bookkeeping classes and worked as a bookkeeper until he retired. Eze was even a qualified *shochet* (ritual slaughterer). In addition, he formed a partnership with Hilda's brother Benny and they supplied the Sassoon Mills with textiles and chemicals.

After the establishment of Israel in 1948, Eze also became involved in immigration work. He helped arrange passports for Jews wanting to emigrate from India, and his work gained him the nickname 'Eze Passport'. Eze and his sister-in-law Sarah were instrumental in helping hundreds of Jews immigrate to Israel, the UK, Canada and Australia. These included Eze's two sisters who immigrated to the United States in October 1953 and his brother Mordy, Mordy's wife and their five children who immigrated to London in the 1960s.

Eze and Sarah's work was all legal and they received payment for it. But the work was more than just a job for them; they genuinely wanted to help members of their community. Eze knew the then Commissioner of Police and was therefore able to expedite the travel documents of the Jews wanting to leave Bombay. Both Sheila and Mozelle distinctly remember trying to get to sleep at night while their father prepared passport applications and documents in the same room with the lights on.

This was in a country and in an era where children's needs were not paramount the way they seem to be in much of the West today. Sheila and Mozelle simply tolerated the lit room without a word of complaint. They knew there was simply nowhere else for their father to work and that their discomfort was insignificant compared to the important work he was doing.

Education

Judaism was paramount in the Jacob household. Eze ensured that his children learned to read Hebrew, and learned all the *Shabbat* and festival prayers and all the Friday night *shbachot* (hymns), by employing a Hebrew tutor. He also took his children to the Magen David Synagogue every Saturday morning.

On Saturday afternoons, Sheila and Mozelle (and when he was old enough, Fred) went to Bnei Akiva meetings at the Synagogue Compound where they socialised with Jewish friends and listened to a Jewish history *shiur* (lecture). In fact, Sheila learnt all her Jewish history at BA, as well as learning about the weekly *parsha* (Torah portion) and *Rashi* commentaries on the Torah portion. After the *shiur*, there was singing and Israeli dancing.

Sheila also went on BA camps twice a year, each May and December, to the Indian towns of Matheran and Mysore. There, she spent time with her Jewish friends and had intensive learning experiences focusing on Judaism.

Despite the Jacob family being strongly affiliated with the Jewish community, Eze refused to send his two daughters and only son to the Sir Jacob Sassoon Free School. Rather, he sent his Jewish daughters to The Convent of Jesus and Mary (a Catholic school), and his son to Christ Church (a Christian school), both in Byculla. Although a few Jewish children attended the Catholic and Christian schools, they were in the minority. Nevertheless, Eze, a religious Jew, preferred to send his children to these schools because he considered the standard of education to be higher than the free Jewish school. He always stressed the importance of a solid education and didn't want his children to end up like many of the other Baghdadi Jews who didn't go to university, or worse still, didn't even finish school.

His philosophy was that education was the most important thing he could give his children, equally for his daughters as for his son – even if he had to pay for it. The Catholic school fees weren't particularly high as they were subsidised by the Indian Government. Still, it was obviously more expensive than the Jacob Sassoon Free School.

Eze's belief in the importance of a good education meant that school and learning were the defining features of Sheila's life in Bombay. In addition to attending school five days a week, Sheila and Mozelle had three tutors come to their apartment after school for extra lessons. They had one tutor for Hindi, another for Hebrew and a third for music. The piano tutor came on Sunday mornings and the Hebrew tutor came late on a school night – around 8.00 or 9.00 p.m. – and Mozelle remembers wishing he'd arrive earlier as her eyes burned reading the fine Hebrew print.

On school days when there was no tutor coming, Sheila would come home from school, do her homework and read books. She never went to the Synagogue Compound in the evenings to play with the other Jewish children, as Eze wouldn't let his children go there after school. The only time Eze allowed his children to play in the Synagogue grounds was during school holidays.

In fact, Sheila rarely had the chance to do anything frivolous because Eze was so focused on education and insisted that her studies come first. If Sheila did well at school sport relays and was asked to come back for training, Eze would never allow her to go. And although Eze had no hesitation in hiring tutors to supplement his children's education, he didn't consider it important that his children be taught to swim or to ride a bike. This failing is something my mother has always regretted.

Even where Bnei Akiva was concerned, Sheila's involvement was not unrestricted. Sometimes friends would ask Sheila and Mozelle to come to a function outside of the regular Saturday afternoon meetings. Sheila would reply that she was too scared to ask her father if she could go along.

So the BA friends would go over to Sheila's apartment and ask Eze, 'Uncle Eze, can they come?' (the term 'uncle' was a sign of respect for elders rather than an indication of family ties). Usually, Eze would respond in a strict voice: 'No, they're not allowed to go,' although sometimes, if he was in a good mood, he would let his daughters go with the other children. If a BA group was going to the movies and Sheila's friends asked Eze's permission to take Sheila and Mozelle with him, Eze would enquire in a stern voice, 'What type of movie are you going to see? Who are you going with?' He was always concerned about what his children were doing and with whom they were spending time.

It seems to me that Eze's focus on his children's education, particularly that of his daughters – although somewhat extreme – was very enlightened for the particular community in which he lived. When he passed away many years later, one of Eze's former neighbours commented that Eze was really ahead of his time in the way he ran his family. In some ways, this is true. In my view, Eze's greatest strength was his determination to achieve his goals and do what he perceived to be the best by his children, even if that ran counter to what his peers were doing and even if it meant significant personal sacrifice on his part.

21. SHEILA'S BOMBAY CHILDHOOD

Despite his strictness, Eze did allow his children some fun and entertainment: the cinema. Eze loved to go to the movies, and he and Hilda had season tickets. Every Sunday evening they went to the cinema, usually the Excelsior near VT (Victoria Terminus) Station, to see Hollywood movies.

Eze frequently took his children to the movies too, but he would only allow such frivolity on the weekend. When Sheila and her siblings were young, Eze took them to see films with Charlie Chaplin, Laurel and Hardy, Dean Martin and Jerry Lewis, and Danny Kaye. They saw classics like *The Sound of Music* and *My Fair Lady*. Sheila loved it.

However – and this to me characterises my grandfather in a nutshell – Eze would always leave the cinema five or ten minutes before the movie ended so that he could catch a taxi before the crowds exited the cinema. So he and his family always missed the end of the movie they had gone to see! Living in Los Angeles years later, Mozelle recalls that one of the movies she had seen in the Bombay cinemas was on TV and she had always wondered what happened at the end of it. She only finally found out when she watched the televised version!

The other treat Eze allowed was the occasional outing for ice-cream at 'Jai Hind' in the Bombay area of Nana Chowk. Sheila recalls the ice-cream at Jai Hind being fabulous, especially the peach melba – her favourite.

The great irony of Eze's firm parenting, however, was that his one lapse caused Sheila an enormous amount of grief in later years.

Although Hilda and Eze insisted their children brush their teeth each night, they regularly indulged the children with lollies or chocolate *after* the teeth brushing and didn't make the children clean their teeth again before bed. As a result, Sheila suffered much pain and expense in the dentist's chair. I distinctly remember my mother's insistence that my brother and I clean our teeth twice daily as children so that we wouldn't 'end up with teeth' like hers.

Although they never played in the Synagogue Compound after school, the Jacob children did play with the other Jewish children who lived in their apartment building. Like the Benjamins, my mother and her siblings had few material possessions. In fact, my mother had no toys at all until her father's sisters, who had immigrated to the US, sent Sheila and Mozelle a tea set and some dolls. By this time, Sheila was already six years old. She treasured the toys, particularly the tea set.

Having so few toys meant that Sheila and her friends used their imagination to improvise games. They played inside their building and outside their apartment with cigarette packets, marbles and tops, and played hopscotch, and hide and seek. They also read a lot and made up word games.

In Bombay, material possessions were simply unimportant and unaffordable. Sheila rarely got any new clothes, except a few dresses at *Rosh Hashana* (Jewish New Year), which lasted her until the following year. Like the precious few toys she had, she cherished each new dress.

Sheila recalls that nothing in Bombay was thrown away if there was any possibility of repair or re-use. For example, when the wicker wore away on the wicker chairs in Sheila's home, the chairs were not discarded. Instead, the wicker was simply replaced. When the cotton filling on their pillows wore out, the *pinjara wallah* came to re-fluff the cotton with a *pinjara* (a string in a wooden frame; the cotton fluffed up as the string was pulled).

Sheila was once given books about Catholicism by some of

the girls at her Convent School in an attempt to convert her from Judaism. She had no interest in conversion but instead of throwing the books away, she sold them – in true Indian style – to the *channa wallah* to make money. The channa wallah, who sold hot *channa* (dried roasted peas) in paper cones, used the pages from the books to make more of the paper cones.

This no-waste approach remains in both my parents' blood. They look after their possessions in a way that only those who have once had nothing can do. My children have inherited my old toys, books and even placemats, which my parents have managed to keep in pristine condition despite being decades old. I have seen this aptitude for preservation in other Indian families too. It seems to be a hallmark of having once lived among so much poverty where even the smallest item is of some value.

Despite the restrictions placed on her by her father and her lack of material possessions, Sheila enjoyed a happy childhood living in her parents' home. She was rich in family and friends, and had much joy in her life. Sheila remembers with particular fondness the treats which were always awaiting her arrival home from school: the aaya would make *chapatis,* or Hilda would buy cake from the cake wallah, or the *bhel puri* wallah would come and they would eat *bhel baal* in the evening.

However, both my mother and my aunt Mozelle commented independently to me that their childhoods were very sheltered and they consequently grew up very naïve. One thing Sheila was not protected from was the knowledge that her future did not lie in Bombay, or even in India. Before she was even ten years old, Sheila knew that one day – although she didn't know exactly when – she would be living in the United States of America.

22. FAREWELL BOMBAY: THE JACOBS

Although Sheila was seventeen years old before her family actually left India, she was aware for many years prior that she would eventually be leaving India. Sponsored by Eze's eldest sister Thelma (who had immigrated to the US in 1953 with Eze's other sister Emily), Hilda and Eze had their visas issued even before their youngest child, Fred, was born in 1957. However, Eze postponed his family's departure from India after Fred was born and he continued to delay it for a number of years.

Eze's brother Mordy immigrated to London, but Eze preferred Los Angeles to London because he didn't want to live in the cold, wet London climate. And although other Baghdadi Jews immigrated to Israel, Eze didn't want his children subjected to compulsory Israeli army service, so he didn't consider Israel a viable relocation option. Fortunately, Eze was financially secure enough that he was able to choose to immigrate to the US: immigrants were required to have a certain amount of money so they wouldn't rely on the government for support, and without that sum, a visa would not be issued.

Early in 1966, Eze and Hilda were advised that they had been on the US immigration list for too long and if they didn't leave Bombay within a specified time frame of approximately three months, they would be taken off the list and their consent to immigrate to the US would be revoked.

Although it was a difficult decision, Eze resolved that it was finally time to leave Bombay. He was already fifty-two years old by then – no longer a young man – and there were many unknowns.

Would he be able to find work? If so, what kind of work would it be? Sheila speculates that her father waited so long to leave India because he wanted her, his eldest child, to be in a position to help financially support the family if it became necessary. Which it did.

It wasn't long after Eze made his decision that he and his family left India for the United States. Within three short months, Eze had to arrange for the leasehold on their Bombay apartment and its furniture to be sold, pack the family's entire belongings and wind up his business supplying the Mills. It was an exceptionally busy time.

To complicate matters, only two months before the family's scheduled departure, the Indian rupee was devalued by 55 per cent. This devaluation had the practical effect of halving the value of Eze's assets, which was hardly an ideal way to start life in a new country. Interestingly, despite his apparent ambivalence about leaving India, Eze later wrote (in an autobiography he typed after persistent requests by my Aunt Mozelle, which in the end amounted to only two pages), 'This tremendous loss did not deter me to leave India for the welfare and prosperity of my children.' Eze had always known there was no future for his children in India and he was not going to give up the opportunity to give them a better life, despite the vastly reduced amount of money he would bring to America.

Eze, of course, did not make this decision in consultation with his children. When Sheila was first told that the decision to leave India had been made, she found it difficult to believe she was finally going, even though she'd known for years that this had been her father's plan. Nevertheless, she felt an enormous sense of relief that she was leaving, despite having begun a Bachelor of Arts degree at St Xavier's College only six months earlier.

Once Eze decided the family would be leaving Bombay for LA, he persuaded Sheila to discontinue her degree course and do something 'more practical'. This amounted to a bookkeeping course at Bamji's College and learning how to operate a switchboard. Both were well below what Sheila was capable of achieving, but unfortunately, her dreams and potential accomplishments were not high priority compared to the need to get out of India and survive in the US.

Despite its impact on her education, Sheila was glad to be leaving Bombay. This was because in the preceding months and years, most of her family and friends had left. First her Uncle Joe's family, who had lived next door, left for Israel in 1951. The vacant apartment was filled by Uncle Sayeed's family. They too emigrated to Israel in the late 1950s, as did Uncles Isaac and Benny and their families. Uncle Mordy and his family left for London only months before Sheila and her family left Bombay. One of Sheila's best school friends emigrated to London and another school friend left for Israel. And Sheila's Saturday afternoon Bnei Akiva youth group meetings had become smaller and smaller as more and more Jewish families left Bombay.

The disintegration of her community left Sheila feeling anxious and unsettled. All her friends were leaving and she was concerned that she would be left behind. Sometimes she woke up in the middle of the night in a panic. Now, finally, she was leaving too.

Mixed with this sense of relief was a feeling of apprehension, as Sheila would be moving to Los Angeles, California: a strange city where she had no friends. She had no idea what to expect. All she really knew was that her living conditions would be greatly improved and that she would have more material possessions; she knew she would be able to go into a department store and buy many of the things that were simply unavailable in Bombay.

However, as a seventeen-year-old who had never travelled outside of India, and indeed, who had never travelled further than the southern Indian destinations of Mysore and Bangalore on camping trips, Sheila could not possibly anticipate what everyday life in Los Angeles would be like. Similarly, Sheila's sister Mozelle remembers sitting at school in Bombay and daydreaming about life in LA when in reality, she had absolutely no idea what to expect.

It was 25 July 1966 when Sheila and her family finally left Bombay. They left by a Japan Airlines Flight and stopped overnight in Tokyo. It was necessary for them to fly via Tokyo so they could take advantage of the time difference and gain an extra day – they arrived in the United States only one day before their visas expired.

Tokyo marked Sheila's first night ever in a hotel room. It also gave her a glimpse of life in a Westernised city: her family did a half-day city tour in Tokyo and Sheila recalls being amazed by the city. The pace of life was so fast, the skyscrapers so tall and the technology so advanced – worlds away from Bombay where so little was mechanised due to the availability of cheap labour.

The Jacob family were greeted at Los Angeles International Airport by Eze's sister Thelma and her husband Allen. Los Angeles would turn out to be a difficult city for all of them, but particularly for Sheila. Sheila's parents, sister and brother eventually called Los Angeles home. But my mother Sheila was never able to do so.

23. LOS ANGELES, USA

When Sheila arrived in Los Angeles she was in a state of shock. The transition from East to West was an enormous culture shock and Sheila felt completely disoriented. She went from the insularity of her small Byculla Jewish community – where neighbours were an integral part of everyday life – to the anonymity of LA's San Fernando Valley. Sheila spent her entire first two days in LA in tears.

Sheila's sister Mozelle found the transition difficult too, and in Mozelle's early weeks in LA she cried every day. Unlike Sheila, Mozelle had not yet finished school. She entered 9th grade in LA, but found it difficult to settle in. She missed her Bombay friends enormously.

During their first six months in Los Angeles, the Jacob family lived with Eze's sister Thelma's family in the suburb of Van Nuys. Given their apartment in Bombay had no refrigerator, no washing machine, no telephone and they had no car, it was a massive change to move to Thelma's large house – complete with swimming pool.

The existence of large shopping centres and the consumer culture of the United States was also a huge difference between Bombay and LA. Mozelle remembers the time she went on the escalators at the 'mall' – her very first time – and feeling like she was going to fall.

Another of Mozelle's early memories of LA is a Sunday lunch at Thelma's house. Sheila and Mozelle were used to having big Sunday lunches in Bombay of pomfret, rice and *zalata* (chopped salad of tomato, cucumber and fresh coriander). On that particular Sunday in LA, the sisters were made one peanut butter sandwich each for lunch. Mozelle was still hungry. So she asked for a second peanut butter sandwich. She was still hungry. So she asked for a third and was met with a peculiar look which seemed to say *who on earth eats three peanut butter sandwiches in one sitting?* Mozelle hadn't yet learned how things were 'done' in this new country.

On another occasion, soon after she arrived in LA, Mozelle was asked if she wanted a hot dog. What was a 'hot dog'? Mozelle wondered, confused by the unfamiliar expression. She'd never had anything remotely like it in Bombay.

Sheila similarly remembers the divide between India and America. When Sheila first arrived in the Valley, Thelma's neighbour earnestly enquired whether Sheila had ridden an elephant to school in Bombay and why she spoke English so well. Sheila was flabbergasted by the neighbour's ignorance. But she realised that in the same way as she had been unable to imagine life in America while she was living in Bombay, the Americans she met had no clue about the culture and lifestyle she had left.

At first, Sheila's family were welcomed into Thelma's home. However, there was soon a lot of friction as a business venture which Eze and Thelma entered into turned sour. This situation made Sheila and Mozelle miss Bombay and their friends even more.

After their six months in Thelma's home, the Jacobs moved into their own apartment on Victory Boulevard, where Eze and Hilda remained for eighteen years: the entire time they lived in LA. Both Sheila and her mother Hilda found life in the so-called City of Angels far from heavenly. Hilda, by then in her late forties, didn't work when she first arrived, which intensified her feelings of loneliness. The only people she knew in the entire city were her two sisters-in-law and their families, plus a friend of hers from

Bombay and a friend of Eze's from Rangoon. She cried often, alternating between wanting to go back 'home' to India, or to 'the land of my brothers' – Israel – where her beloved brothers and their families now lived. Hilda deeply missed the family-oriented and community-focused life she had led in Bombay.

Perhaps most importantly, there was no established expatriate Bombay Jewish community in the Valley which the Jacob family, as new immigrants, could join. Very few of India's Baghdadi Jews emigrated to the United States due to the stringent economic requirements demanded of potential immigrants.

And, although there was a large Iraqi Sephardi Synagogue in Santa Monica, it was a 45-minute drive away – too far to drive on a Saturday morning after a busy work week. LA was extremely sprawled out compared to the confines of the Baghdadi community of Bombay which they had just left and this increased Sheila's sense of isolation.

There was a vast difference between daily life in Bombay and in Los Angeles. In Bombay, everyone's apartment doors were kept open and neighbours dropped in and out of each other's homes. The women cooked food and swapped recipes and tastings of their latest dishes, and the children played together after school. Everyone in the community knew each other and socialised together. It had been an easy, innocent life in India.

In LA, both Hilda and Sheila felt they no longer belonged to a community. Rather, they each felt isolated and alone. Eze and his two younger children, Mozelle and Fred, had easier transitions from Bombay to LA as they integrated into American society via work and school.

But Sheila, who'd already finished school, and Hilda, who was home all day, keenly missed the company of their Bombay friends and neighbours and found the transition very difficult. In LA, Hilda didn't even know her neighbours, let alone have them visit. Like my paternal grandmother Hannah's experience in Sydney, my maternal grandmother Hilda was very bored in her early months and years in the US.

Sheila too had little contact with people her own age. She went from what she fondly describes as a 'rich, vibrant society which was very Jewish' to 'virtually nothing'. She did make an effort to meet people by taking American History classes at the local college and driving to the Fairfax area for Israeli dancing classes, but she found it very difficult to form friendships like the ones she'd had in Bombay.

In Bombay, Sheila had felt tied to the Jewish community, but her life in Los Angeles was much more secular. This was due in large part to the different structures of the Jewish communities in Los Angeles and Bombay.

Around the same time that Sheila and Mozelle were adjusting to their new lives in LA, the geographical distribution of Jews in the United States was becoming more decentralised and suburban, due to a decline in immigration.[42] Also, American Jewish communities at the time were beginning to show rising assimilation rates. For example, a study of Jewish marriages in Washington DC in the 1960s indicated that only one per cent of first generation Jews married non-Jews, but ten per cent of second and eighteen per cent of third generation did so.[43]

The decentralised nature of Jewish communities in the United States meant Judaism was a much stronger force in Sheila's life in Bombay than it was in Los Angeles. This was despite the fact that, as a percentage of the population, there were significantly more Jews living in LA alone than in the whole of India at the time Sheila arrived in LA: in 1971, the Jewish population of India was 15,000 out of a total of just over 511 million, with most Jews living in Bombay. The entire Jewish population of India was therefore an almost negligible proportion of the total population.

At the same time in the US, the total population numbered just under 200 million, of which 550,000 Jews lived in Los Angeles. Jews living in LA were also only a tiny proportion of the American population at the time. Still, their proportion was 93 times greater than the number of Jews relative to the Indian population.

In part, the difficulty which Sheila had in adapting to American life was that her family's Baghdadi Sephardi traditions were not widely practised in the Valley. As there was no Sephardi synagogue close to their home, the Jacob family became members of an Ashkenazi synagogue called Mishkan Israel. It was located on Victory Boulevard and was within walking distance of their apartment.

Used to the Sephardi way of prayer, an Ashkenazi congregation and service were foreign to Sheila because Sephardi and Ashkenazi synagogue services – both prayers and tunes – are very different. Sheila clearly remembers one of the older men in the synagogue lamenting: 'If you don't speak Yiddish, what kind of a Jew are you?' Indeed, many of the Ashkenazi Jews with whom Sheila came in contact in LA were not even aware of the existence of Jews in India. Sheila never experienced any hostility from these Jews, but she did feel that she never belonged.

Yet despite the differences, Eze became an accepted member of the Mishkan Israel congregation and went to synagogue regularly. At the same time, his transition to life in LA was by no means smooth.

Over fifty years old at the time and with no local experience, Eze found it hard to find employment in LA. It was difficult for him too to immigrate to a strange city with a completely difficult culture. Sheila recalls that although her father never showed much emotion, it was undoubtedly a difficult adjustment for him.

But Eze kept busy in his role as provider for his family, and once in LA, he never looked back. It simply wasn't his personality to dwell on things he couldn't change. (Many years later, when

I asked Grandpa Eze whether he had ever wanted to return to Bombay after he'd arrived in LA, he responded brusquely, 'What's the use of talking about then? Talk about today!')

In order to earn a living, Eze went into partnership with his sister Thelma and her husband only months after he arrived in LA. Together they bought a car wash business named Sultan Car Wash, located in Van Nuys. However, the venture wasn't successful and Eze lost a significant 65 per cent of all his savings when he co-owned the business between 1966 and 1968. The fallout from the car wash saga was so bad that Eze and Thelma refused to even speak to each other for many years afterwards.

After selling the carwash, Eze worked as a bookkeeper. Although he had never driven a car in Bombay, Eze travelled long distances for work on LA's busy freeways. It was very different from anything he had ever known, but he did not complain and simply took it in his stride.

Sheila worked at the car wash too for about six months, do-ing the books and as a cashier, but she didn't enjoy it much and soon looked for a different job. Unlike Abe's experience in Sydney, Sheila found it hard to find work in LA – one job she applied for had 600 applicants, so it was much more competitive than Sydney's job market. But then, via word of mouth, she heard about a job in the computer department at Lanfield, a wholesale liquor company, and she secured that job. She would have to drive to her new job and was very excited to buy her own car – her first car ever – albeit second-hand. Sheila still has fond memories of her blue Dodge Dart.

As for Hilda, she didn't work in LA at first. But after Sheila resigned from the car wash, Hilda started working there part-time, job sharing the cashier's role with her sister-in-law Thelma. Later, after Eze sold his share of the car wash business to Thelma, Hilda worked as a cook at a convalescent home on Victory Boulevard, only a five-minute walk from home.

While Hilda was working at the convalescent home, she enrolled in a dietitian's course at LA Valley College. Once she completed the course, Hilda worked at the convalescent home as a dietitian for the remainder of the time she lived in LA, a total of fifteen years. She woke up at 5.00 a.m. every morning, five days a week (with Friday and Saturday off) and walked to work, her shift finishing in the early afternoon. On Fridays she prepared for *Shabbat* and while she was working on Sundays, Eze did much of the housework (the laundry and shopping) while Sheila, Mozelle and Fred cleaned the house.

It was a dramatic change to her life in Bombay, but Hilda loved her work and being outside the confines of her apartment. She had been very lonely at home on her own so she was thrilled to be around other people. And so, although it took Hilda some time to adapt to life in LA, she eventually adjusted and thrived there. Eze too adapted and ended up embracing life in LA and the opportunities it provided him.

However, the transition from Bombay to LA proved too difficult an adjustment for Sheila to make. My mother has no regrets about leaving Bombay as she acknowledges that, despite her happy childhood, the city was dirty and overcrowded and it held no future for her. But she distinctly remembers feeling trapped in LA. Sheila readily admits that there were many material advantages to American life. In LA, her family had possessions she could only have dreamt of while living in Bombay. Goods like a washing machine, dishwasher, car and ready-made clothes. She vividly recalls her first Christmas in LA, going down an escalator in a shopping centre and seeing what she describes as 'fairyland'.

But for Sheila, the material goods, although initially impressive, never filled the emptiness of her Los Angeles life. After three and a half years, Sheila couldn't bear living in LA any longer and felt she had to leave.

24. A SOJOURN IN ISRAEL

Anxious to get out of LA after she lost her job at Lanfield due to a merger, Sheila decided to go and live in Israel for a year. She got another job in North Hollywood and worked hard and saved everything she could to pay for the trip. But it wasn't easy for her to save money: Sheila was responsible for contributing towards the rent on her family's apartment and she also had the expense of running her car, including driving lessons.

Sheila had actually taken driving lessons while still living in Bombay. But the lessons, in typical Indian style, were a little chaotic. Sheila's teacher used to take her driving in Crawford Market where she had to detour around cows and goats. Suffice to say it was necessary for her to take additional lessons before she started driving in LA!

Sheila attempted to go to Israel twice before she actually left, but both times, her father Eze pressured her to change her mind. He was not at all in favour of his eldest daughter leaving home. In his usual pragmatic and direct manner, Eze said to Sheila, 'If you go to Israel, who will you marry? A farmer?' Yet finding a husband was the last thing on Sheila's mind at the time. She just wanted to get out of LA – as soon as she could.

The third and final time Sheila planned her escape from LA, she booked her airline ticket to Israel and enrolled in a five-month Hebrew language course at Ulpan Etzion (Hebrew language school) in Jerusalem. Sheila didn't discuss her plans with her father as she knew he would again make it difficult for her to leave. She didn't have anything arranged for the seven months after *ulpan*; she would work it out while she was in Israel.

Sheila only bought a one-way ticket from LA to Tel Aviv but left enough money with her parents to pay for her ticket home from Israel. By not buying a return ticket from the outset, it was as if Sheila somehow hoped she wouldn't have to go back to the US – although she had no idea how such a possibility could eventuate.

Mozelle, very close to her older sister, was devastated when Sheila told her she was going to Israel. Mozelle decided that she too wanted to go along, but was told that she had to be eighteen years old to enrol in *ulpan*. Mozelle cried constantly after Sheila left because she missed her sister so much. It was only after Sheila left that Mozelle found out that she only needed to be sixteen to have joined her sister. But by then, it was too late.

Sheila was extremely excited about her first visit to Israel. She wanted a new beginning and was looking forward to meeting up with family and friends from Bombay who had moved there. At the same time, she was very sad to leave her siblings to whom she was so close. Her mother understood, and told her to go and be happy. This I can imagine, as my grandmother Hilda only ever wanted everyone she loved to be happy. And Sheila was not happy in LA.

In December 1969, twenty-one-year-old Sheila Jacob left Los Angeles for Israel.

Ulpan Etzion was the first *ulpan* in Israel and was established in 1949. It is still in operation and is located in the neighbourhood of Baka in south Jerusalem. Today, however, only new immigrants to Israel between the ages of twenty-two and forty-five who hold a degree from a tertiary institution can attend Ulpan Etzion.

Had such criteria applied in 1969 when Sheila arrived as a tourist, she would never have been able to attend. But when Sheila's course commenced in January 1969, all the students in her class were tourists. They came from every corner of the world – thirty countries in total – including South America, France, England, Australia and Canada.

Sheila had a great time at *ulpan*. She lived in the dormitory there and made a lot of friends. Hebrew classes were held six days a week (every day except Saturday) from 8.30 a.m. until 1.00 p.m. This meant Sheila had free time every afternoon, a lot of which she used to tour around Jerusalem. She also spent some afternoons working, cleaning the home of famous Israeli pianist Yosef Tal who then lived in Jerusalem's Jewish quarter.

Ulpan classes finished early on Fridays in preparation for *Shabbat* and Sheila usually spent *Shabbat* with relatives and friends. She travelled all over Israel; she had aunts and uncles in Tel Aviv, Ashkelon, Haifa and Eilat and friends in Jerusalem. Most Friday afternoons she travelled by bus to Bat Yam, a suburb just outside of Tel Aviv, to visit her Uncle Benny and Aunty Sarah's family – the same Uncle Benny her father had been in business with in Bombay.

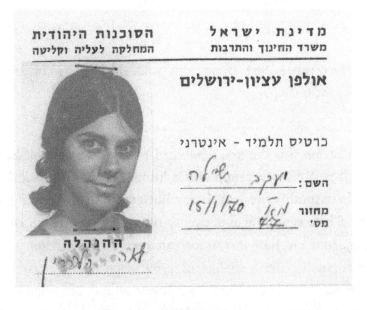

Sheila's Ulpan Etzion ID card

142

Although she missed her immediate family in LA, Sheila was thrilled to be surrounded by familiar faces again. She loved being in Israel as she was constantly seeing people who had been part of her Bombay community. In Israel, she again found the sense of community which she had found to be so lacking in Los Angeles.

Some of the people Sheila met in Israel had left Bombay many years before her and she barely remembered them. But even if their faces weren't familiar to her, their names certainly were. And the relatives she spent *Shabbat* with cooked her delicious Iraqi food which she always looked forward to. *Hamim* was a staple on the *Shabbat* lunch menu at Uncle Benny's home in Bat Yam.

On the Fridays evenings Sheila hadn't travelled to be with relatives, she went to the *Kotel* – the Western Wall – with friends from *ulpan*. It was a 45-minute walk each way from Baka to the *Kotel* but a whole group of people walked down together every week after *Shabbat* dinner. Shlomo Carlebach, the San Franciscan 'dancing rabbi', was there a few times and Sheila describes the atmosphere as absolutely magical. Carlebach sang Hebrew songs at the *Kotel* and the crowds sang, clapped and did Israeli dancing while he sang.

Not only was it great fun but Sheila recalls feeling an enormous sense of freedom. Spirits were high as it was not long after Israel's victory in the Six Day War of 1967 and prior to the 1973 Yom Kippur War. There were only a handful of soldiers patrolling the *Kotel* and Sheila describes the general atmosphere in Israel at the time as 'euphoric'.

After the *ulpan* course finished in June 1970, Sheila got a job at Bank Leumi, in the Rechov Yafo (Jaffa Street) Jerusalem branch, only minutes away from the Old City. While at *ulpan*, Sheila had learnt a basic level of Hebrew but was not fluent. For many years, I had assumed that since my mother had worked in an Israeli bank following her stint at *ulpan*, she had achieved fluency in Hebrew. I was quite impressed by this achievement. It was only later that I discovered that Sheila's position at Bank Leumi was in the foreign exchange department and that she didn't speak Hebrew at work at all. The bank wanted her for her English language skills, not her Hebrew!

Once *ulpan* concluded, Sheila could no longer live in the dormitory and had to find alternate accommodation. Sheila and her French *ulpan* roommate Cecile looked for an apartment they could rent together. After only a few days of searching, they found a place in Arnona, in Ramat Rachel. A Yemenite family occupied the upstairs apartment, while Sheila and Cecile occupied the two-bedroom apartment downstairs. Their balcony overlooked the whole valley of Jerusalem and at night they could see the *Knesset* (Parliament building) all lit up. It was, Sheila recalls, absolutely spectacular.

However, their apartment was quite isolated and was the penultimate stop on the bus route to Ramat Rachel. Despite this, Sheila felt incredibly safe. From Ramat Rachel, Sheila was able to walk down through fields and past Arab labourers to another bus stop on Derech Bet Lechem. The bus to Ramat Rachel stopped in the evening but the bus to Derech Bet Lechem ran until midnight, so if Sheila returned home late on Saturday night from visiting relatives she caught that bus and walked home late at night through the fields with no fear at all.

Sheila has been back to Israel as a tourist numerous times since she lived in Jerusalem after *ulpan* and has never had the same feeling of security as she did in 1970. Looking back, she is incredulous at how safe she felt in Israel at the time.

She also felt very free in Israel after feeling so constrained and isolated in Los Angeles. She admits that it was quite daunting at times because she was on her own, but she did have a lot of extended family in Israel. Yet in spite of having a wonderful time, Sheila never really considered staying in Israel because she greatly missed her family, especially her sister Mozelle and brother Fred.

Even though Sheila disliked Los Angeles, her plan continued to be to return there at the end of her year away. Yet by December 1970, she was nowhere near Los Angeles. In fact, she never lived in Los Angeles again.

25. SHEILA AND ABE

While Sheila was living in Israel in 1970, she corresponded regularly with her family in Los Angeles. She also wrote to a few members of her old community from Bombay, including Abe Benjamin, who was living in Sydney, Australia.

In early 1970 in Sydney, Reuben Shellim, a friend of Abe's from Bombay – the same friend he had travelled by boat with when he emigrated to Australia from India – suggested that Abe meet Sheila in Israel. 'What are you doing here?' Reuben asked Abe. 'Sheila's in Israel and that's where you should be.' Abe's eldest brother Benny agreed that Abe and Sheila might make a good match.

Sheila and Abe had a mutual relative through marriage: Sarah Levy (she was Sheila's aunt and Abe's mother's niece). Abe's brother Benny wrote to Sarah, suggesting the possibility of a match between Abe and Sheila. Sarah approached Sheila with this information and Sheila replied that Abe should write directly to her if he was interested in seeing her in Israel.

Abe admits to feeling some pressure to get married at this time. He was twenty-six years old, getting closer to twenty-seven, and although he'd settled well into Sydney life he had no marriage prospects on the horizon.

Abe's younger brother Sammy was engaged to marry in December 1970 and his younger sister Mabel would be married in January 1971. Once Sammy and Mabel married, only Abe, his seventeen-year-old brother Isaac and their mother would be living in the Brighton Boulevard house.

If a relationship with Sheila didn't work out, a trip to Israel would at least provide Abe with a much needed holiday as he was under a lot of pressure at work in Sydney. It would also be an opportunity to visit his sister Elaine and her family, and to catch up with his friends from Bombay who had emigrated to Israel.

Nevertheless, the decision to go to Israel was not one which Abe made easily. At the same time as the prospect of meeting up with Sheila surfaced, an opportunity arose for Abe to buy an apartment. Acutely aware of how precious little money he had, Abe wanted to create a secure financial future for himself. But ultimately, what he really wanted was a family of his own and he knew that buying the apartment would not provide him with that. Abe was faced with the choice of using his limited funds to buy property in Sydney, or travelling to Israel. He chose Israel.

So in June 1970, Abe wrote to Sheila to let her know he was coming to Israel to visit his sister Elaine and her family, and that he wanted to meet up with her. He acknowledged that they had been apart from some time and had been living in different countries, but he did say that he had intentions to marry and thought Sheila might be suitable. But in order to save enough money and get time off work, Abe would not be able leave Sydney for Tel Aviv until late October 1970.

This created a dilemma for Sheila. If she waited for Abe to get to Israel, she would miss her only sister Mozelle's wedding in Los Angeles in August 1970. Sheila was extremely close to her only sister and she had already missed her brother Fred's bar mitzvah while she was in Israel. But Sheila only had enough money for a one-way ticket from Tel Aviv to LA. So she couldn't afford to go back to LA for the wedding and then return to Israel. She had to choose: either she waited for Abe and missed Mozelle's wedding, or she returned to LA and tried to make a new life for herself there. Sheila took a gamble and waited for Abe. Mozelle, on the other hand, was tremendously disappointed that Sheila wasn't at her wedding.

Abe arrived in Tel Aviv on 28 October 1970. He stayed with his sister Elaine and her family, and a few days later he went to Jerusalem to meet Sheila. By this time, Abe hadn't seen Sheila in over three years. He spent three consecutive days with her in Jerusalem and proposed to her within two weeks of his arrival in Israel. He proposed without fanfare, in his characteristically humble style. He simply said, 'I don't have much money and don't have any property, but will you marry me?'

Sheila had dated a couple of Israeli men in Israel, but none of them interested her. She had also dated a couple of men in LA, but none of them seriously. Although she was not in love with Abe at the time he proposed to her, Sheila accepted Abe's proposal immediately and agreed to start a new life with him in Sydney.

Abe too was not in love with Sheila at the time he proposed. But he had known her since childhood, knew she came from a good family and knew that they had a common background. He wrote to Sheila's father Eze seeking his permission to marry Sheila and took his chances that love would grow after they married.

This is quite a foreign concept to me. I asked my parents individually why they didn't simply decide that they were interested in spending more time together and then see if they wanted to get married. Both gave me the same response: that to wait and see if love developed was a luxury they could not afford. Abe could not stay in Israel for much longer than a month; Sheila had no money to remain in Israel past December 1970 and their background made it unacceptable for them to live together before they married. They both agree that they took a huge risk, particularly my mother. But both are adamant the risk paid off.

Interestingly, none of Abe's brothers and sisters were shocked or surprised by Abe and Sheila's engagement, and Sheila's family were equally accepting. Admittedly, some of Sheila's friends in Israel were stunned at her decision to move to Australia. But their concern was more materialistic: Abe had proposed to Sheila without a ring, and the astonishment of Sheila's friends was that she would move to a strange country at the other end of the world, a place where she had no family, without even a ring, jewellery or gifts to entice her over. (And yet, in 2011, my parents celebrated their fortieth wedding anniversary and they have had a happy and loving marriage.)

Sheila agreed to marry Abe because she felt they had a strong bond and good sentiment between them. Abe appealed to her because he was very family oriented. She knew he was gentle and caring, that his father had died when he was only young and that he was devoted to his mother. She knew Abe had remained in Bombay when all his immediate family had left in order to pack up the family's belongings and sell their apartment. Clearly, he was responsible. Although they hadn't been close friends in Bombay, Sheila had known Abe since her Bnei Akiva days when he was a *madrich* (youth leader) and she knew that he was a trustworthy person.

In addition, Sheila didn't really want to return to LA and Abe's proposal provided her with an opportunity to go to a new place and start a new life. She chose not to concentrate on the 'what ifs' which crept into her mind, deciding she would give it a try. Her intuition told her it was the right thing to do. She stresses that God, luck and fate were with her.

Sheila readily admits that she was nervous about moving to Australia: she had no family and no friends in Sydney. In hindsight, Sheila acknowledges that her Israeli friends may have been right. 'Maybe I was crazy,' she says now, laughing. But she adds that it all happened so fast there wasn't much time to be scared.

And in reality, Abe and his family were no strangers to Sheila. Although Sheila had no guarantees that their marriage would be successful, she did know that she and Abe shared similar values and the same Iraqi Jewish heritage. Sheila had found she had little in common with the American men she met in LA. Abe had a similar experience with the women he met in Sydney. Although Sheila and Abe had different upbringings in Bombay, they came from the same community and therefore had significantly more in common with each other than with Australian and American Jewish men and women their age. The five-year age gap between them was not an issue.

After Sheila accepted Abe's proposal, they travelled around Israel together for four days. They based themselves at Abe's sister Elaine's home in Tel Aviv. Although Sheila hadn't met Elaine before, she did know Elaine's husband Ellis; he was an electrician who had done all the electrical work in Sheila's family's apartment in Bombay. The Baghdadi community of Bombay really had been an intimate one, where everyone was somehow connected to each other.

On 6 December 1970, Sheila left Tel Aviv for her new life in Sydney. She never returned to live with her family in Los Angeles. Sheila's sister Mozelle will never forget the day she found out Sheila wasn't returning to LA but was moving to Australia. It had never even crossed Mozelle's mind that Sheila wouldn't return to LA after her year in Israel and Mozelle was devastated. Sadly, the two sisters, although exceptionally close, have never lived in the same country since Sheila left the United States for Israel in 1969.

26. WELCOME TO THE FAMILY

Abe had booked his ticket back to Sydney from Israel months before proposing to Sheila. His ticket home included a stopover in India so that he could go to Agra; despite having lived in India for twenty-two years, Abe had never seen the Taj Mahal. Sheila would have liked to accompany her fiancé, but she couldn't afford to, so she flew direct to Sydney. Ironically, Abe never ended up seeing the Taj Mahal on his way home from Israel due to an air strike in Delhi. Despite all his years in India, my father was fifty-six years old when he finally visited the Taj Mahal for the first time.

Abe's detour via India meant that when Sheila arrived in Sydney on 8 December 1970, he wasn't even there to greet her. But he made sure that his bride-to-be was well looked after until he arrived the following day. Abe's eldest brother Benny and eldest sister Florrie picked Sheila up from Sydney airport after her long flight. Sheila hadn't met Florrie before, but she did know Benny because Benny's then-wife had been Sheila's neighbour in Bombay.

Both Benny and Florrie were very welcoming, as was Sheila's future mother-in-law, Hannah. In fact, Sheila was welcomed by the entire Benjamin family and was immediately accepted into Abe's family. Granted, Sheila already knew many of the Benjamins from Bombay: Benny, Margaret, Mabel, Sammy and Isaac. But she'd never met Florrie or Sass.

Sheila's first impression of the Benjamin family was that they were warm and friendly. In her early days in Sydney, while the other Benjamins were working, Hannah acted as Sheila's tour guide. Hannah took Sheila to the city and showed her Sydney's famous landmarks such as the Harbour Bridge, as well as the big department stores David Jones and Nock and Kirby. Sheila was taken with the beauty of her new home city; it was much more attractive to her than LA's San Fernando Valley.

Between arriving in Sydney in December 1970 and marrying Abe in April 1971, Sheila lived with Abe's sister Florrie and her family. It would have been unacceptable for her to live with Abe before they married. So for four months, Sheila lived with Florrie, her husband Charlie and their two daughters – who, until the moment she met them, had been complete strangers. Sheila was welcomed into their home, even though it was only a small two-bedroom apartment. In the warmth that characterises Indian-Jewish families, Sheila clearly remembers Charlie telling her that his family was her family too, and that she should treat their home as if it were her own.

The bond that Sheila formed with Florrie's family in the four months that she lived with them remains even now. In 1976, Sheila and Abe bought a house around the corner from Florrie and Charlie's apartment. They continue to live a two-minute walk away from each other today.

While Sheila was living at Florrie and Charlie's, Abe visited her almost every evening after work. Often, they walked down to the beach together. But Abe soon tired after his long days at work and never stayed late. After he left, my always-energetic mother worked on knitting him an intricate cable-stitch jumper. It was a present to him before they married and he wears it even now, almost forty years later.

Since both Sheila and Abe had run out of money, it was vital that Sheila find a job as soon as possible. Sheila laughs now when she recalls how incredibly broke they both were. Abe had spent all his money on his trip to Israel and Sheila used all of her money (which she had put aside for her return ticket to LA) to buy her ticket to Sydney.

During Sheila's first week in Sydney, she applied for two jobs. Since she had left India on a British passport and retained that passport, she was automatically entitled to live and work in Australia. Sheila was offered both the jobs she applied for and was surprised at how quickly and easily she was able to find employment, especially compared to her experience of finding work in Los Angeles. But Sheila's Sydney salary was only half of what she had been earning in LA.

Sheila accepted a job as a statistician in the NSW Department of Education in the city. There were no computers at the Education Department so all Sheila's work had to be done manually, mostly on an adding machine. It was the stereotypical government job: Sheila wasn't encouraged to work hard during her eight-hour day, and in addition to a lunch hour, she was given breaks for morning and afternoon tea. She was told not to finish her given tasks in a hurry, and when she left after only four months because it was so slow and boring, she was replaced by two people. How times have changed!

It was only some years later, in 1979, that the railway line from Bondi Junction to the city was completed, so Sheila commuted to the city by bus. Although the distance was only around ten kilometres, the journey took a whole hour. Luckily, Abe often picked Sheila up in his company van on his way home from work on Sydney's north shore. And the Sephardi Jewish network operated to help out too, with Charlie's cousin often giving Sheila a ride to the city in the mornings.

Finally, Sheila again felt part of a community. She had no relatives of her own in Sydney and Sydney's Sephardi community was different from the one she'd left in Bombay, but Sheila was comfortable living in Sydney. Moving to Australia had been the right decision.

Sheila and Abe's Engagement and Wedding

Abe and Sheila's engagement party was held on a Sunday afternoon on St Valentine's Day 1971, in Hannah's home at 88 Warners Avenue, Bondi. Hannah had moved from Brighton Boulevard to Warners Ave in 1969 because her home was going to be demolished in order to build a block of apartments.

The engagement party was an informal affair and the forty guests primarily consisted of members of Abe's immediate family. The Benjamin sisters and sisters-in-law prepared all the food for the party themselves (food preparation was outside the domain of the Benjamin males). The women made traditional Iraqi and Indian snacks like chutney sandwiches, *chat patay*, spring rolls and *aloo bhaji*, plus cakes for dessert.

Abe followed the Iraqi *soonayi* tradition, whereby the groom-to-be's family gave the bride-to-be a piece of jewellery (in this case, a pair of gold earrings) and a tray of lollies to make their engagement sweet. It was a lovely tradition which unfortunately is rarely practised anymore.

Between their return from Israel in December 1970 and their Sydney wedding in April 1971, Sheila and Abe worked hard to save money for their wedding. Still, they could hardly afford an extravagant wedding. Sheila borrowed her sister Mozelle's wedding dress and her sister-in-law Mabel's veil. The bridesmaids wore the same dresses they had worn to another sister-in-law, Kathy's, wedding. And Sheila and Abe paid for their wedding themselves, as Sheila's parents had lost a lot of money in the car wash business in LA and Abe's mother Hannah had many children and little money.

Sheila's mother Hilda and sister Mozelle travelled from LA for the wedding. Mozelle initially didn't think she'd be able to attend her sister's wedding. She had married only seven months earlier in LA and she and her new husband, in her words, 'had nothing'. But they scraped the money together and Mozelle surprised her sister, writing Sheila a letter which included the question: 'What colour dress do you want me to wear to your wedding?' When Sheila received the letter, she squealed with excitement and delight. It had been almost eighteen months since she'd seen her sister.

However, Sheila's father Eze and brother Fred were noticeably absent. In hindsight, neither Hilda nor Mozelle could explain why Eze didn't attend his eldest daughter's wedding. He was certainly healthy enough to travel and he could have afforded the airline ticket if he'd really wanted to. Sheila's view is that he didn't want to have to endure the long flight to Sydney and to take his youngest child, Fred out of school.

While Mozelle was in Sydney for the wedding, she also stayed at Florrie's house, even though there wasn't really enough space in the apartment. But Mozelle insisted she would sleep on the floor if that meant she could be close to her beloved sister. The Bombay way of life was not so far behind them that living in such close quarters was problematic. They wouldn't have wanted to do it permanently, but in the lead up to the wedding, all of them living in Florrie's apartment was a lot of fun.

Although the custom among Baghdadi Jewish brides in Bombay was to have a henna night prior to their wedding with food, music and skin decoration, that custom wasn't widely practised once the Baghdadi Jews left Bombay. So although Sheila's mother Hilda and Abe's eldest sister Florrie both had henna nights in Bombay, Sheila didn't have one in Sydney.

On 25 April 1971, Sheila and Abe were married at Sydney's Sephardi Synagogue by Rabbi Simon Silas. Sheila was twenty-two years old; Abe twenty-seven.

Sheila and Abe's Sydney wedding was more formal than weddings had been in their former Bombay community. In Bombay, the tradition was to hire a hall, have music, friends, ice-cream and chips, followed by a big meal at home which the family prepared themselves. In contrast, Sheila and Abe's wedding reception was held at the Maccabean Hall in the Sydney suburb of Darlinghurst with fewer than a hundred guests and kosher catering. The wedding was a simple one, yet a lot of fun with much dancing to celebrate the *simcha* (happy occasion).

As the months and years went by, Abe and Sheila grew to love each other. Sheila especially loved Abe's giving and forgiving qualities. 'Love grows,' she says. 'The most important ingredient [of a good marriage] is mutual respect and tolerance.'

At the same time, however, Sheila never really got to know her mother-in-law Hannah. My mother found, just as I did while I was growing up, that she wasn't close to her because Hannah wasn't someone you could get close to. But my mother was always grateful that Hannah never interfered with her and Abe. Indeed, Hannah never interfered with any of her children, even while they were bringing up their own children, her grandchildren. In stark contrast to the stereotypical Jewish mother, it simply wasn't Hannah's style to meddle.

Sheila and Abe's wedding was the third Benjamin wedding in a period of four months: Sammy married in December 1970; Mabel in January 1971; Abe and Sheila in April 1971. Each of their wedding photos, all taken in black-and-white in the same spot at Sydney's Sephardi Synagogue, used to sit side by side on the wall in Nana's lounge room.

Although Hannah was happy to see three of her children married in such a short time, it was very difficult for her when all her children moved out of her home. Sammy, Abe and Mabel moved out within a few months of each other. Five years later, Isaac, the youngest of the Benjamins, moved out when he married.

So great was the adjustment at this time that Hannah had a nervous breakdown. Her life had revolved around her children for so many years and without a husband for companionship, she found that she was unable to be on her own.

But ever-resilient, Hannah eventually recovered and got used to living alone. She became incredibly independent and self-sufficient. Indeed, Hannah became so independent that many years later, when she was physically unable to look after herself, she argued vehemently with her children that she wanted to continue to live on her own rather than moving to a nursing home.

27. BONDI LIFE

In the late 1960s and early '70s, the Sydney beachside suburb of Bondi was very different from the way Bondi is today. Twenty-first century Bondi is much more cosmopolitan, busy and expensive than it was forty years ago. It was where you lived if you wanted to be in the Eastern Suburbs – the heart of the Jewish community – but couldn't afford the more affluent suburbs of Dover Heights or Rose Bay or Bellevue Hill. When my father first arrived in Australia in 1966, Bondi was a developing, middle-class suburb. It wasn't at all the glamorous, desirable area it has since become.

There were barely any shops in Bondi when the Benjamins first arrived in Australia and not even a shopping centre in nearby Bondi Junction. (The first shopping centre didn't open in Bondi Junction until the early 1970s; Bondi Junction Plaza followed in 1976; both were replaced by the mammoth Westfield complex in 2003–04.) Chain supermarkets didn't exist and, in fact, when Nana first arrived in Sydney, she used to order fruit and vegetables from Dooleys, a cart on Chambers Avenue, Bondi. Her order was delivered to her front door, in a manner not unlike what she'd been used to in Bombay.

The few shops that were around closed early, except on Thursday nights when they were open until 9.00 p.m. Only the small corner shops – known as 'milk bars' – regularly stayed open late so people could buy bread and milk. Everything was shut on Saturdays after midday and all day on Sunday. Sunday was a day for going to church – even the pubs were closed!

When my mother arrived in Bondi in 1970, she was shocked by

how quiet it was and by the slow pace of life. On Campbell Parade –
the street which runs parallel to Bondi Beach – there were no cafés
at all and only a few takeaway food shops. Sheila describes the area
as 'completely dead' after 5.30 p.m. It was very different from what
she'd been used to since leaving Bombay – in both Israel and LA,
shops, restaurants and cafés were open late and on weekends.

But the fact that there were so few shops and that they were
closed on Sundays, meant there was more time to spend with
family and friends. In their early years of marriage, my parents
regularly spent summer Sunday afternoons with the Benjamins
at Bondi Beach. Of course, no Benjamin family outing would be
complete without food, and everyone contributed something to
a communal picnic lunch – *aloo* (potato) *bhaji,* sandwiches and
summer fruit such as watermelon and cherries. The summer days
were often hot, but the temperature was usually cooled by evening
thunderstorms, bringing welcome relief from the heat.

They were good times, both Sheila and Abe recall. Like in
Bombay, they had few possessions and finances were tight. But
they had each other and the company and support of the wider
Benjamin family, which by this time had expanded to include
numerous grandchildren – Abe and Sheila's nieces and nephews.

Sephardi Synagogue

Like her husband and in-laws, my mother also became involved
in Sydney's Sephardi Synagogue. When Sheila first arrived in
Sydney, the then-president of the Synagogue's Ladies Auxilliary,
Sally Morris, was looking to get some of the younger women in
the community involved. Sheila and her sisters-in-law joined other
young women in the community to form the Ladies Guild, an
offshoot of the Ladies Auxilliary. When Sally Morris passed away,
the women she had trained up took over the running of the Ladies
Auxilliary.

A large part of the role of the Ladies Auxilliary was organising and catering for functions held at the Synagogue. This meant my mother and aunts helped cook for *Shabbat* morning *kiddushes*, fetes and food fairs. Indeed, my mother honed her cooking skills via her involvement in the Ladies Auxilliary.

At the time, Sydney's Sephardi community was quite a melting pot of members from varying countries of origin. Each nationality brought their own traditional recipes to the Synagogue kitchen.

The Egyptian Jews, for example, cooked different food from the Baghdadi Jews. On one occasion, Egyptian-born Mrs Danon made falafel and Florrie's husband Charlie arranged (via his work in the bakers' section of the Department of Labour and Industry) to buy pita bread to accompany it. Although there are numerous falafel shops in Bondi today, falafel in pita was quite a novelty in those days in Sydney's eastern suburbs.

Another time, the Sephardi women were given a demonstration as to how to bake *hamantaschen* (a biscuit traditionally eaten on the festival of *Purim*) with a date and walnut filling. *Hamantaschen* were new to the Baghdadi Jewish immigrants, but they gladly added it to their cooking repertoire, embracing the familiar ingredients of dates and nuts in place of the jam or poppy seed filling commonly used in Ashkenazi kitchens.

In this way, the Sephardi Synagogue kitchen connected the community's women. Food played a central role in all the functions held by the Synagogue and the Ladies Auxilliary gained a reputation – which stands until today – for cooking delicious Sephardi food.

Due to their involvement in the Synagogue, the Sephardi community formed the basis of my parents' social lives in Sydney, in a similar way as it had done in Bombay. Certainly, the organisation of social functions was more formal in Sydney than it had been in Bombay, but that was in large part due to the structure of Sydney life.

Social events in Bombay were arranged on a more ad hoc basis because daily life in India was more relaxed. The help of the aayas and the fact that everyone lived in such close proximity to each other allowed arrangements to be made spontaneously. In Sydney, however, the community was more spread out geographically. And its members' home and work lives were significantly more hectic and demanding than they had been in India. Plus there was the issue of finances: the Bombay community was funded largely by the Sassoons, but Sydney's Sephardi community had no such financial backing. Events such as fetes, bingo nights, food fairs and games evenings were scheduled throughout the year to raise money for the Synagogue.

In this way, Sydney's Sephardi Synagogue played a central role in my parents' lives from the time each of them arrived in Australia. It continues to do so today and the Sephardi community provides my mother and father with an invaluable support network and source of friendship. Not to mention many contemporaries with whom to discuss the ongoing and highly charged topic of Synagogue politics …

Just before they married, Sheila and Abe had taken over the lease of the apartment Hannah had been living in on Warners Avenue. In turn, Hannah and Isaac – the only one of her children still living with her – moved to a smaller apartment on O'Brien Street, Bondi.

In 1972, Sheila and Abe bought an apartment on Brighton Boulevard. Ironically, it was in the exact location of the property that Hannah and her children had rented when they first arrived in Sydney. (That property was knocked down and a block of apartments was built in its place after Hannah moved out.)

When I was born in October 1974, twenty-six years to the day after my mother Sheila's own birth, my parents were still living in that Brighton Boulevard apartment.

PART 4

BONDI

28. MY MOTHER'S SPICE CUPBOARD

I was one and a half years old when my parents and I moved from Brighton Boulevard to a semi-detached house on O'Donnell Street in Bondi. In 1978, not long before my fourth birthday, my brother Michael (then Mikey, now Mike) was born. In Sydney, our parents lived and brought us up very differently from the way they had grown up in Bombay.

My parents' home has always been their castle. Having each grown up with so little in the way of material possessions, they both worked hard to be part of the Australian dream of owning their own home. My brother, cousins and I spent hours playing in our backyard and riding our tricycles up and down the long concrete driveway which ran along the side of our house. When we got older the long, rectangular-shaped driveway formed the perfect replication of a cricket pitch, which kept Mike, an aspiring cricketer, entertained for hours.

Not especially interested in playing cricket, I loved to spend time looking through my mother's cookbooks. Food was a central part of our lives and my mother could regularly be found cooking up delicious meals and snacks in the kitchen.

Unlike Nana Hannah, my mother hadn't been cooking since she was a teenager. In fact, she never cooked when she lived in Bombay or when she lived in Los Angeles. In Bombay, Grandma Hilda and her cook prepared all the meals. And by the time she lived in LA, Mum would have liked her mother to teach her to cook, but Mum's and Grandma's schedules were such that my mother was never home when Grandma cooked: during the week

Grandma left for work early and cooked after she got home in the early afternoon. But at that time of day, my mother was still at work. Grandma never cooked on *Shabbat* and when Mum was home on Sundays, Grandma was at work.

So my mother only learnt to cook after she married. My parents couldn't afford to eat out which meant Mum always cooked at home. Even if they had wanted the odd takeaway meal, my parents' observance of the laws of *kashrut* (the Jewish dietary laws of keeping kosher) made it difficult, given there were few vegetarian options and not a single kosher establishment.

Dad, although used to his mother's extensive repertoire of dishes, did not demand such cooking skills of his new wife and never compared Mum's cooking to Nana's. Yet my mother, always the perfectionist, practised until her cooking skills were at least respectable.

Ironically, my mother rarely ate spicy food while she was growing up in India. While she was living with her future sister-in-law Florrie prior to marrying my father, she watched Aunty Florrie – a great cook in her own right – prepare many Indian dishes. When Mum was introduced to Aunty Florrie's cooking – the spicy curries and *pilafs* and *bhajis* – she immediately fell in love with them. Mum learnt from Nana too, although Nana tended to cook more Iraqi-style food which was less spicy than the Indian food which Aunty Florrie made.

After she married, Mum often stopped at Nana's on her way home from work, told her what she wanted to make for dinner and then asked Nana for the recipe. My mother preferred to cook simple food rather than intricate dishes, as she simply didn't have the time that Bombay housewives and their aayas did to prepare dishes like *coobas* or *mahashas*. Mum admits there were a few disasters, but she was motivated to experiment and perfect her skills.

Over the years, Mum developed a love of cooking and her own

style independent of both Hannah and Florrie. She progressed to become a superb cook, able to prepare both traditional Iraqi and Indian dishes and more multicultural food such as pasta and couscous-based meals. My mother is also a talented baker, skilled at making Baghdadi specialties such as *kakas* (ring-shaped biscuits), date *babas* (biscuits filled with dates) and cheese *samoosas*. But even today, Mum still uses Nana's recipe whenever she bakes fruit cake.

By the time my brother and I were born, Mum had mastered the cooking of many traditional Indian meals: curries, *shiftas* (minced meat patties shaped like small sausages, flavoured with onions, herbs and spices) and vegetable dishes like *aloo bhaji*.

Spices have always been an essential component of my mother's cooking. But neither my brother nor I liked spicy food much when we were children, so Mum often made two versions of the same dish: a spicy one for her and Dad, and a mild one for Mike and me. Despite my lukewarm attitude to eating the spicy food, I still loved to peer inside my mother's spice cupboard, with its aromatic smells and vivid colours.

The cupboard my mother used for storing spices during my childhood didn't look like much from the outside. In fact, it was the smallest cupboard in the kitchen, perched almost out of reach on top of the copper range hood above the stove. But that small spice cupboard housed a vast array of powders, seeds and pods.

The spices weren't stored in fancy containers. Reminiscent of the lollies that Nana Hannah stored for her grandchildren in an old Moccona coffee jar, Mum's spice cupboard was full of old Kraft peanut butter jars and ETA mayonnaise containers. Originally holders of everyday pantry staples, they became the home of her most used spices: cumin, coriander, garam masala, turmeric and paprika. The less used or more potent spices – chilli powder, cloves and cardamom pods – were stored in smaller jars which originally contained spreads like jam or honey.

Inside each jar was a miniature spoon. The spoons were usually white ones which had been attached to the jelly cups which my brother and I bought from the milk bar across the street from our house. While the plastic cups were discarded as soon as we finished our jelly, my mother carefully saved the plastic spoons for her spices.

My mother taught me the names of all her spices, so she could ask me to get out the mustard seeds from the cupboard for her *aloo bhaji*; tamarind for her *chat patay* (chickpeas and potatoes in tamarind sauce); fish curry powder for her fish curry; or agar powder and rose essence for her signature dessert, rose *agar agar* (jelly made from seaweed powder).

As a child, I couldn't reach the spice cupboard without standing on a chair. Once on the chair I was able to sort through the various jars and examine the appearance of some of the lesser used spices. I remember trying to work out a way of distinguishing chilli powder from paprika, which looked almost identical to my six-year-old eyes. I eventually worked out that the two spices had different smells, but I was always careful to double-check that I hadn't mistakenly pulled out chilli powder when Mum wanted paprika.

Along with the spices, my mother bought huge five-kilogram sacks of basmati rice – a household essential – for her cooking. Our pantry also contained jars of *brinjal* (eggplant) pickle and packets of pappadums. Bottles of rose-flavoured cordial for watermelon sherbet, atta flour for *chapatis* (flat bread) and *kewra* essence for kulfi. There were always curry leaves on hand, harvested from the curry-leaf tree in our garden. And a seemingly endless supply of *kotmir* (fresh coriander) in the fridge, which Mum used in everything from salads to curries.

Mum and Nana (and all the other Sephardi women) bought their spices from Eze & Son, a Jewish-owned spice shop in Brighton Boulevard, Bondi – the same street Nana first lived in when she moved to Australia.

The shop was originally started in the 1950s by Kelly Moses in his garage and was one of the few places at the time – and possibly the only place – where fresh spices and kosher food could be bought.[44] Kelly Moses was a Baghdadi Jew originally from Burma and he was a spice trader there before emigrating to Australia from Bombay in 1949.

Kelly's business soon outgrew his garage and expanded into a grocery store on Brighton Boulevard run by his son Eze. The shop was named 'Eze & Son', although its customers often referred to it as 'Eze Moses'. The shop did well and in the 1960s Eze expanded the business and began importing spices, pickles and Indian groceries such as rice, chickpeas, lentils and pappadums.

The import side of the business was well-established by the time Nana Hannah arrived in Sydney. By then, Eze Moses owned the whole apartment building above the shop too, as well as other property on Brighton Boulevard. In fact, the first home Nana rented in Sydney was owned by Eze Moses.

Eze was a religious Jew and observed *Shabbat*, so his shop was closed on Saturdays. However, he opened on Sundays, even though most other retail outlets in Sydney at the time were closed.

Each Sunday, Indians came from all parts of Sydney to this Bondi spice shop. In fact, a former Indian colleague of mine told me that when she was a child, her family used to make the trip to 'Eze Moses' all the way from Newcastle – some three hours away by car – to buy spices and groceries. The shop was very popular because Eze Moses sold what no one else did: fresh spices. Business was so good that people used to double park their cars on Brighton Boulevard on a Sunday in order to get inside.

Today, the building that used to house 'Eze & Son' is a yoga school. I have been to yoga classes there but to me, the site always reminds me of my childhood and shopping with my parents for spices and pickle and my favourite rose-flavoured cordial.

29. GROWING UP BENJAMIN: SYDNEY

I had a wonderful childhood. We lived only a ten-minute walk from Bondi Beach and spent summers swimming, playing in the sand, going for walks on the promenade and eating delicious gelato.

My childhood revolved largely around the world of the Benjamins. With my father's brothers and sisters all living nearby (except for Aunty Elaine and her family in Israel), I had lots of cousins my own age to play with and a large extended family. My aunts' and uncles' houses were my second homes and I went to kindergarten and school with many of my cousins.

We saw the extended Benjamin clan regularly. There was our weekly Saturday night visit to Nana's house, plus there were always picnics and barbeques being organised. Each featured plentiful amounts of food, a game of cricket (both televised and a live, Benjamin alternative) and lots of noise and laughter.

The English spoken when we all got together was peppered with a few Hindustani and Arabic words, but whole conversations could be conducted in Hindustani if the adults didn't want the kids to understand what they were saying. However, we soon learnt to recognise and understand the important words: the terms of endearment and the swear words. We were lovingly referred to as *jani aini* (Arabic for 'light of my life'), *abdalak ana* (Arabic for 'you are my love') and *kalaija katookra* (Hindi, literally 'a piece of my heart' meaning 'part of me').

The wider Benjamin family provided a warm and loving environment in which to grow up, albeit a boisterous one in which one almost had to shout to get heard. The Benjamin siblings had such fun childhoods themselves that when they had their own children, they took the opportunity to be kids again. Without exception, the five Benjamin brothers remained kids at heart.

Uncles Sammy, Sass and Charlie (Florrie's husband) were always the ringleaders when it came to joking around and mischievous activity. My brother Mike, the youngest of Nana's nineteen grandchildren, was often the target of their energies.

Uncle Sammy in particular liked to *shawoosh* (stir up) my brother. Mike was easily provoked and a reaction from him, whether it was tears, laughter or shouting, was almost guaranteed. When Mike was six years old, Uncle Sammy decided he wanted to buy cricket pads and gloves for the young cricket aficionado. He phoned Mike and instructed him to get the measurements of every finger on both of his hands, together with various leg measurements (ankle to knee, ankle to groin) on both of his legs. When Mum tried to gently explain to Mike that it wasn't necessary to measure *all* ten fingers on his hands, he started shrieking, insisting that 'Uncle Sammy won't be able to buy me the gloves and pads unless I give him all of the measurements!' Uncle Sammy laughed with glee (and not without a hint of triumph) when he heard how seriously his nephew had taken his instructions.

Elana and Mike, 1981

As wonderful as my childhood was, it was also a very conservative upbringing. Even in Sydney, my parents were bound by the traditions and culture of the Baghdadi Bombay community. My brother and I were raised with what are now considered to be old-fashioned values: respecting elders simply because they are older (not because they earned respect), never answering back to parents and going to synagogue regularly.

It was difficult for my parents, especially my mother with her strict upbringing, to raise their children in a country and society so different from the one in which they grew up. Even the standards of the wider Jewish community of which we were a part were not as stringent as my parents' values. I was faced with conflicts similar to those faced by others whose parents have emigrated to a new country: living and being educated in a society that valued competitiveness, materialism and individualism, and a home life that stressed family, community, respect and religion.

As for the wider Benjamin family, its members like to cast males and females into gender specific roles wherever possible. The world of the older Benjamins is one where the women cook while the men sit and wait to be served; where girls are groomed for marriage, children and keeping house.

While I was growing up, I often felt that the major concern of my Benjamin aunts and uncles was that my cousins and I, particularly the females, get married. Not that they weren't concerned about other aspects of our lives like how we were doing at school and our friends. But it was instilled in me at an early age – without actually being spoken – that family was the most important aspect of my aunts' and uncles' lives. Marriage was the first step in adding to the Benjamin clan.

So for years, well-intentioned Benjamins would ask not-so-innocent questions about my social life, like 'how's your love life?'

and 'do you have a boyfriend?' And at all family *simchas* (joyous occasions), especially weddings, the older Benjamins always singled out the unmarried Benjamins for special attention.

It is customary at Jewish weddings for the bride and groom to drink wine from a *kiddush* cup. But there is always some wine left over because the bride and groom rarely have more than a few sips each. That leftover wine was always reserved for the unmarried Benjamins to drink from.

'Come here,' Uncles Sass and Sammy, or Aunty Florrie, would command. 'Drink the wine,' they instructed, ignoring the obvious unhygienic nature of all of us sharing the same cup. It was never worth arguing, however, so my cousins and I dutifully followed the superstitious practice. Once each of us had swallowed our sip of wine, they would proclaim the four-word Sephardi-Iraqi-Benjamin mantra: 'Please God by you'. They were blessing us that we too would reach the ultimate aspiration of being a bride or groom under the *chuppah* (Jewish marriage canopy).

My own parents were well aware of my enormous distaste for such comments. They were more concerned about my education anyway, wanting to give me opportunities to study and have a career in a way they were never able to. And they sent me to a private Jewish day school where the emphasis was on getting high enough marks to guarantee a place at university and then progressing to become a professional.

My father, even though he was so thrilled I graduated from university with a law degree, could never understand why I didn't want to become a barrister or even to practise in a law firm. He didn't realise in the way I did that there was no way to reconcile being a practising lawyer or barrister and being a Benjamin. How could I have and take care of a family of my own if I was at work for most of my waking hours?

Of course, I am not only part of my father's family, but of my mother's family too. Until I was ten years old, my mother's parents – my grandparents Hilda and Eze Jacob – lived in Los Angeles. They

Hilda and Eze Jacob, Los Angeles, 1982

existed solely on the periphery of my life; only entering my world for a few weeks at a time every few years when we went to visit them in LA.

I am Grandma Hilda and Grandpa Eze's second grandchild

out of a total of only four grandchildren. Grandma and Grandpa loved my brother and me dearly. But it was difficult for us to form a strong bond with our maternal grandparents when we were small children because we lived so far away from them.

Despite our regular visits to LA, Grandma and Grandpa never visited us in Sydney. Grandpa Eze didn't even attend my parents' wedding, so I suppose it wasn't likely that he was going to fly to Sydney for a holiday.

And as this was the 1970s – minus email, Facebook and Skype – Grandma and Grandpa were far removed from my daily life. Phone calls to the USA were extremely expensive then, so I rarely spoke to them. In fact, I had little contact with Grandma and Grandpa other than the birthday cards they sent me each year. My parents did record audio tapes of my brother and me as preschoolers, singing and talking to them, but I don't recall them sending us any tapes back or even letters. Perhaps that is why I never wrote to them either.

Consequently, I have few childhood memories of Grandma Hilda and Grandpa Eze. But from the photos of our holidays to LA, I can see that they adored having their grandchildren come to visit: in every picture they are positively beaming. Nevertheless, the three- or four-week block we spent in LA every few years was hardly conducive to spending quality time with Grandma and Grandpa. I was much more interested in playing with my cousins (Aunty Mozelle's children) when we went to LA than visiting my grandparents.

I vaguely remember Grandma and Grandpa's Van Nuys apartment, 'Margo Villa', but I don't recall that they had any toys for us to play with. I do, however, clearly remember being dragged by my parents, kicking and screaming, from my cousins' home to visit my grandparents. Seeing them was an obligation rather than a pleasure because they were so unfamiliar to me.

In spite of my stubborn refusal to engage in much dialogue or play with Grandma, she always smothered me in hugs and kisses and called me her 'lovey dovey'. And Grandpa Eze was the only grandfather I ever knew, so his role was a special one, even though I never got to know him well.

But then, when I was nine years old, my grandparents emigrated to Australia from the United States. That was at the end of May 1984. By that time, they had lived in the US for close to twenty years. Not a short amount of time. And they were no longer young; in fact, they were both already retired. At the time they moved to Sydney, Grandpa was seventy years old, Grandma sixty-two.

Although it was a move they chose and one which meant the twilight years of their lives were lived relatively independently and among their native Baghdadi community, Grandma and Grandpa never really accepted Sydney as their home. To me, even though they ended up living in Australia for almost as many years as they lived in LA, their hearts always remained in Los Angeles' San Fernando Valley.

30. GRANDMA HILDA AND GRANDPA EZE

Grandma and Grandpa moved to Sydney after my uncle, their youngest son Fred (and Grandma's undisputed favourite child) emigrated to Australia. Uncle Fred had moved to Sydney one year earlier after deciding he didn't want to continue studying medicine. Aunty Mozelle, her husband and two children intended to follow to be with the rest of us in Sydney.

But things don't always work out as planned. Although Uncle Fred anticipated moving to Sydney on a permanent basis, he returned to LA after spending only two years there. And when Uncle Martin (Mozelle's husband) was unable to find a job he was happy with in Sydney, his family's plans to emigrate failed to materialise. But Grandma and Grandpa were too old to move back to LA, so they remained in Sydney. In fact, they spent the rest of their lives there – eighteen years in total.

For years, my maternal grandparents had lived halfway across the world. Suddenly, they were almost around the corner, less than a ten-minute walk away in a large apartment on Military Road close to Bondi Beach.

Now that they lived so close to us, we had Friday night dinner with my grandparents almost every week, alternating between their place and ours. It was mostly over these *Shabbat* dinners that I got to know my Grandma Hilda and Grandpa Eze.

Grandma and Grandpa were the proverbial chalk and cheese. He was serious, she was jovial. He was strict and domineering, she was gentle: a peacemaker. He was frugal, she would gladly have given all her money and possessions away to those she loved and to the needy. He was extremely organised, she was easygoing and could never say no to anyone. Grandpa Eze was the pragmatist, Grandma Hilda, the dreamer. Sadly, they were ill-suited to each other, yet they endured a lifetime of marriage.

I do not wish to cast judgment on Grandpa Eze, particularly as I never had the benefit of obtaining his views on much of the material in this book. By the time I started my research, Grandpa had begun to suffer from dementia. What I do know for certain is that Eze Jacob wasn't a bad man. He just wasn't suited to Grandma Hilda.

By all accounts Grandpa had mellowed by the time his grandchildren were born, but even in my recollection, everything was either black or white to Grandpa. He refused to entertain even the darkest shade of grey.

What stands out most in my mind about Grandpa is his love of the United States. I can't remember him ever making a negative comment about the US. Grandpa was so enamoured with the US that I often wondered why he stayed in Sydney. Grandma too used to sing the praises of LA.

Grandpa considered the US absolutely wonderful because of the opportunity it gave him to work and establish a new life for himself and his family. Although Grandpa never even came close to being a wealthy man, in the US he was able to gain financial security for himself and for Grandma. Having worked hard as just a teenager to support his mother and younger siblings, financial security was paramount to him. Grandpa and Grandma both worked hard in LA and when they retired they each received a US pension until their deaths.

Grandpa often commented on how advanced Los Angeles was in comparison to 'backward' Sydney, declaring that Australia was 'a poor country'. Uncle Fred used to laugh heartily at the absurdity of his comment. (Surely, Grandpa knew a poor country when he saw one, having lived in India for so many years!) Grandpa insisted that 'it will take Australia at least a hundred years or more to be like America.'

Although he didn't expressly articulate it, what actually impressed Grandpa about Los Angeles was the material aspect of the life he'd lived there. He often mentioned the supermarket coupons which enabled him to buy grocery items at a discount. 'Where else in the world can you do this?' he asked rhetorically. 'Only in America.' Grandpa clearly subscribed to the view that the US is the so-called 'Land of Opportunity'.

Grandma too looked fondly on her time in the US because it was a time when much of her family lived in the same city, particularly her favourite child Fred and her first grandchild Melissa, to whom she was especially close. This family togetherness was vital to Grandma as she was so family oriented.

And so, arguments would rage over our *Shabbat* dinner table in Sydney regarding the apparent virtues of American life. Grandma and Grandpa were always very defensive of America. For years, Grandma lamented the fact that she couldn't buy her favourite breakfast cereal, cinnamon-flavoured Cheerios, in Sydney, only adding fuel to Grandpa's belief that Australia was a 'backward' country.

My mother's view was that Grandma and Grandpa looked at their lives in the States through rose-coloured glasses: she could never understand why they loved LA so much because in her view, they had nothing there. No community and few friends and, once Grandpa stopped driving, little freedom.

Interestingly, Grandma and Grandpa rarely spoke to me about their lives in India. By the time they moved to Australia, they identified more with the US than with India. Whereas the Benjamins reminisced about their 'Bombay days', Grandma and Grandpa reminisced about their 'LA days'.

In reality, Sydney was a wonderful city for both my grand-parents. In their early years in Sydney they were still healthy, and I remember Grandpa diligently doing exercises at home every morning to keep in shape. With the shops and public transport within walking distance, they were able to be independent in a way that would never have been possible in LA.

Grandpa even managed to find some work in Sydney: for a few years he was employed as a *mashgiach* (a supervisor of the *kashrut* status of an establishment or function). Grandpa was also an active member of the Sephardi Jewish community, forming part of Sephardi Synagogue's *minyan* (quorum of ten men required for communal prayers) for many years.

Although they never acknowledged it, Sydney gave Grandma and Grandpa significantly more autonomy and community involvement than they'd had in Los Angeles.

Although I was never very close to Grandpa Eze, I did form a strong bond with Grandma Hilda over the years. She was warm and affectionate, and loved me unconditionally in a way only grandmothers can. She was also quite a character.

Grandma was one of those people who found the good in everything and everyone. Other than the odd complaint about Grandpa, I don't remember Grandma having a bad word to say about anybody. She was almost always smiling and cheerful, and was happiest when all her children and grandchildren were together.

This love of having her family altogether was equalled only by Grandma's hatred of being alone. After all those years surrounded by so many brothers, sisters and extended family in Bombay, Grandma had no interest in spending time on her own. She was very hospitable and loved having visitors, plying them with food and drink at every opportunity. 'Eat, eat.' she would say. 'You look so thin.' And regardless of how long any visitor had stayed, once they announced they were leaving Grandma would invariably lament: 'So soon you're going? You just came!'

Although she spoke English fluently, Grandma tended to revert to Hindustani on a regular basis. Her speech was so divided between the two languages that my brother proclaimed she actually spoke 'Hinglish'. I could understand her short, conversational, phrases, like *egdam aacha* ('very good') and *kya baht karega* ('what are you saying?'). But when she began referencing Persian philosopher Omar Khayyam in Hindustani: *'ye duniya hey musafir khana sub ko hey ek din jana'* (this world is transitory and one day or the other everybody must go), I was completely lost.

Interestingly, I noticed that in the last few years of Grandma's life, she tended to speak Hindustani more often than she spoke English. Hindustani connected Grandma to her early life which had been so happy, and so speaking that language was always a source of comfort to her.

As much as I loved Grandma, I often felt frustrated by her. Grandma had two obsessions in life: marrying off her beloved son Fred and winning the lottery. Both, as far as I was concerned, were a complete waste of time and energy.

As a male – and an unmarried one at that – Uncle Fred got special treatment from Grandma. Regardless of how hard her daughters worked, Grandma constantly ruminated about how difficult things were for her son Fred and frequently referred to him as *bichara* ('poor boy' in Hindustani). The possibility that he never wanted to get married simply didn't enter her mind. Even she couldn't see that it would be better to be alone than to be married and miserable.

Grandma's other favourite pastime was going to the newsagent to buy Lotto tickets. She was always talking about 'winning a million' and dreaming about what she would do with the money. I never had much time for Grandma's Lotto dreams, knowing they were unlikely to come to fruition. What I found wonderful, however, was that although she was intent on winning Lotto, Grandma cared nothing for material possessions. Her dream was to win Lotto so that she could give all her winnings away to the people she loved. In the end, it was Grandma's love of others and disregard for herself that proved her ultimate downfall.

The area over which Grandma and I really bonded was our love of all things sweet. Grandma loved to bake and she often made delicious Iraqi pastries like *kakas*, date babas and walnut rolls, plus good old American apple pie. Grandma always obliged when I called her to ask if she wouldn't mind baking me one of her delicious apple pies. Regrettably, I never thought to ask for her recipe until it was too late.

My strongest memories of Grandma Hilda are of her sitting down each afternoon to her beloved cup of tea and piece of cake, and of the almost choking hugs she gave me each time we saw each other. Even now, in difficult times, I often close my eyes and imagine she is next to me and I am safe, locked in her protective embrace.

Grandma and Grandpa lived in their Military Road apartment for four years, after which they moved to a smaller apartment on O'Brien Street, Bondi. That was the same street on which Nana Hannah lived.

Nana lived in her O'Brien Street apartment – the same one she moved into just before my parents' wedding and the same one that I spent my childhood Saturday evenings in for eighteen years.

In 1989, Nana moved from that apartment after the building owner sold the entire block. But she remained on the same street and moved just a few buildings up to a smaller apartment. And, by complete coincidence, Grandma and Grandpa moved into the same block of apartments in which Nana Hannah lived.

When Grandma and Grandpa first moved into the building, they rented an apartment on the second floor while Nana lived on the floor below. But two years later, an apartment on the first floor became vacant and Grandma and Grandpa moved downstairs. And with that move, remarkably, my three grandparents became neighbours. They could not possibly have lived any closer to one another.

Sadly though, it was as neighbours in this O'Brien Street apartment building that in the space of only a few years, each of my grandparents really aged and became frail.

31. TWIN SISTERS

I was extremely fortunate that at the time I became interested in researching my family's history, Nana Hannah, Grandma Hilda and Grandpa Eze were all still alive and living very close by.

When I started visiting Nana to record her recollections and observations about her life, she was already eighty-eight years old. She lived alone in her one-bedroom apartment in a building situated above Bondi's kosher butcher. Unlike the apartment which Nana lived in while I was a child, I spent little time in this other apartment of Nana's. The Saturday night family gatherings at Nana's house seemed to stop when she moved house. But her change of address wasn't really the catalyst for the change: her children still visited her regularly but as the grandchildren got older, we began to spend the Saturday evenings previously reserved for family with our friends.

Nana had aged immensely since those Saturday nights we spent at her home as children. Although her apartment was only five minutes away from Bondi Beach, she was now unable to walk there. In fact, she needed a walking frame even at home. It was an effort for her to walk from one room of her apartment to another; her back was hunched over and she could only move extremely slowly. She struggled to climb the two steep flights of stairs to the first floor of the building where her apartment was located; and as the months and years went by, those stairs became more unmanageable and hazardous for her. Nana, so used to being so autonomous, was incredibly frustrated by the limitations imposed on her by her ageing body.

Yet she remained fiercely independent, refusing offers from her children to move in with them so they could look after her. And she refused to move into a nursing home and have others take care of her. It was as if moving out of her own home meant giving up her last shred of independence. In reality, she wasn't independent at all anymore, but she was too stubborn to accept that she needed help.

Despite being close to ninety, Nana's face didn't give away her age. Unlike other elderly women, Nana's hair never thinned out but was an attractive, thick, silvery-grey, which she often had pulled back in a headband which showed off her pretty face. Her skin was surprisingly unwrinkled, despite never having used anti-wrinkle

Hannah Benjamin, Sydney, 2000

creams and other beauty products. Even in her old age, Nana was beautiful.

And her memory was incredible. While her body – the same body that withstood eleven pregnancies and gave birth as many times – failed her, her mind remained sharp and agile.

One particular morning I went to see Nana armed with my tape recorder and notebook. Unlike the days of my childhood when Nana used to have whole meals prepared in anticipation of her children and grandchildren visiting, she now struggled to cook just for herself. When I arrived, Nana had just finished cooking herself lunch. 'I can't do this anymore,' she announced. 'I'm too tired to cook,' she continued. 'When I was young I was so speedy, but I'm too old to cook for myself.'

Yet in spite of her comments, Nana had just cooked fish curry from some fresh fish that Uncle Sammy had brought her. She was never one to give up, so instead of cooking a different meal every day, Nana altered her routine and cooked one dish and kept it for two or three days. In later years when Nana was simply unable to cook for herself anymore, her daughters took turns to prepare her food.

Although she had so many children to look after her, it seemed to me that Nana was essentially alone. She had outlived most of her friends who had emigrated to Australia from India around the same time she had. And although her children visited regularly and would do anything for their mother, they had lives of their own. My weekly visits to Nana's were therefore tinged with a certain amount of sadness, because I could see so clearly that she was lonely and unhappy.

Just over a year later, I was on holiday in London on a sort of belated honeymoon with my new husband and went to visit Nana's twin sister, Aunty Sarah.

Despite being twins, Nana and Aunty Sarah had lived apart

for many years by then and their lives had followed quite different paths. Unlike Nana, Aunty Sarah had always worked outside the home; she trained as a nurse in Bombay, and after she immigrated to London in the 1960s, she worked at a company of furriers. With no children of her own, Aunty Sarah and her husband were able to help settle many of the teenagers who came to London from Bombay and their home was always full on *Shabbat* with a huge pot of *hamim* on the table.

Years later, after Aunty Sarah was widowed, she went to live with her brother Hayeem and his wife, Rahma. By the time I visited in 2001, Uncle Hayeem was no longer alive but Aunty Sarah continued to live with Aunty Rahma. Despite frequent bickering, the two women were close companions.

I had met Aunty Sarah before this trip, but it had been some time since I'd seen her. The differences between my grandmother and her twin sister were clearly apparent. Most striking was that Aunty Sarah looked years younger than Nana. Aunty Sarah did have trouble with her vision, but unlike Nana, she moved around with ease and was actually quite agile considering her age. She was quite cheerful, whereas Nana was so frustrated by her body that she rarely smiled. Aunty Sarah was still capable of catching public transport; at that time it was an effort for Nana to go down the two flights of stairs from her apartment to be picked up by one of her children for *Shabbat* dinner.

The disparity between the twins' physical appearance and capabilities wasn't particularly surprising given that Aunty Sarah never had children. Aunty Sarah's body hadn't been subjected to the ravages of pregnancy and caring for children, nor did she have to cope with the grief and stress of being widowed in her early forties.

Yet for all their differences, I couldn't help but notice many similarities between Nana and Aunty Sarah. The most glaring likeness was the sisters' stubbornness. I spoke to Aunty Sarah on the phone before going to visit and she told me that her hearing wasn't very good. When I saw her, I asked Aunty Sarah if she wore a hearing aid. She responded affirmatively, but then admitted that she wasn't wearing it at that time because it was too uncomfortable. Nana too, hated to wear her hearing aid, even though her hearing was so poor that she often didn't hear me entering her Bondi apartment.

Aunty Sarah's hospitality was clearly one of a Baghdadi Jew. She spent the few hours we had with her entreating us to eat. She had prepared *aloo bhaji* but very considerately, not made it too spicy because she wasn't sure if we could 'take the spice'. There was also rice and delicious fried eggplant. No sooner had we finished our last mouthful of lunch that Aunty Sarah offered us tea and fruit. And she later brought out chocolate and insisted that we eat it. Already full, we could only manage a small chocolate bar each. Aunty Sarah was disappointed with our poor effort and instructed us to take the rest of the bag of chocolates home. We refused to take the lot but not wanting to offend her, we agreed to take three bars with us.

Although she was already eighty-nine years old at the time of our visit, Aunty Sarah went on to live for almost another ten years. When she passed away in March 2011, Aunty Sarah was a remarkable ninety-eight years old. The last six years of her life were spent in a nursing home in London. Similarly, Nana Hannah spent the final years of her life in a nursing home. And my other grandparents and Nana's neighbours – Grandpa Eze and Grandma Hilda – spent their final years in the same nursing home as Nana Hannah: Sydney's Montefiore Home.

32. MONTEFIORE

Grandpa Eze

At the same time as Nana's physical health was deteriorating, Grandpa Eze's mental health began to decline. In the initial stages, the loss of Grandpa's memory was so slow that it was almost imperceptible.

Grandpa was eighty-five years old when my mother began to notice that he was beginning to exhibit some unusual behaviour. To begin with, the oddities were not significant, just small things that seemed slightly out of character.

Grandma and Grandpa came over to my parents' home for *Shabbat* dinner every alternate week and one Friday afternoon my mother noticed Grandpa walking up and down our street on his own; Grandma had walked over alone earlier in the day and when Grandpa came later, he wasn't sure which house was ours. At the time my mother didn't think much of it, but in hindsight she realised that this was the beginning of what was later diagnosed as dementia. As the months went past, Grandpa became more forgetful, eventually reaching the point where if he woke up in the middle of the night he wasn't sure if it was daytime or night-time.

Grandpa's decline was very difficult for all of us, but especially for Grandma. In the early months of his dementia, Grandma didn't understand what was happening to her husband and was exasperated by his strange behaviour. But despite their differences, Grandma unquestioningly took on the role of Grandpa's carer, a role she held for almost six years. In addition to the usual domestic duties of cooking, cleaning and washing, Grandma also took on the onerous duties of bathing, shaving and dressing Grandpa each day. It was not easy, particularly given that Grandma was already seventy-seven years old when Grandpa started losing his memory.

Despite the physical demands of caring for Grandpa, Grandma never complained and was always smiling. This, to me, is an indication of Grandma's strength of character. But even with her cheerful disposition and reserves of energy, she could not care for him forever.

When Grandpa became incontinent, my parents and my mother's siblings decided that it was no longer practical for Grandma be his carer. It was time to put him in a nursing home. They chose the Hunters Hill campus of Sydney's Montefiore Home, a well-established provider of aged care to members of Sydney's Jewish community.[45]

Montefiore provided the best Jewish aged care in Sydney, but its campuses in Sydney's Eastern suburbs did not provide the dementia care Grandpa needed. Mum and Grandma would have preferred that Grandpa be closer to home so that Grandma could visit him every day. But Grandpa had to go to Hunters Hill, about a 40-minute drive from Bondi.

Grandma wasn't in favour of Grandpa moving to Montefiore. It was too far away for her liking, and after all their years of marriage, Grandma was afraid to live alone. But there was no choice. Grandpa needed full-time care.

Grandpa Eze was admitted to the Montefiore Home's Hunters Hill Campus in July 2001 and placed in the Lavender Wing Low Care Dementia Unit. He was aware he was going to Montefiore but didn't really understand the implications of the move. When my mother explained to him that he was being moved to the Montefiore Home, he asked her: 'Will I be coming back?'

'No,' she replied, 'because Mum [Grandma] is very tired and needs a rest.'

'Whatever you think is best,' he responded.

But after my parents and Grandma settled Grandpa into his room at Montefiore on his first day there and were getting ready to go home, Grandpa said to Grandma, 'Tell Sheila to pick me up soon.' It was as if the earlier conversation had never occurred.

Nana Hannah

Not long after Grandpa was admitted to Montefiore, my father and his siblings were arranging Nana Hannah's transfer to Montefiore. In the preceding few years, Nana had fallen over numerous times at home and was unable to get herself up. Each time Nana fell, it would take three or four adults – with my father usually being one of them – to help her up. This occurred not just during the day but in the middle of the night too.

Eventually, Nana's children agreed that their mother required full-time care. A full-time carer wasn't a viable option as it would have been too expensive – and Nana would never have agreed to it anyway. The Benjamin siblings eventually decided to move Nana to the Montefiore Home.

Unlike Grandpa who wasn't exactly clear about the effect of his move into the Home, Nana had her full mental capacity. She understood the implications of a move to Montefiore and knew that she did not want to relocate there. Having lived on her own for so long, she was reluctant to give up her independence and her home.

Nana was also worried that none of her children would travel the distance to see her at Montefiore. Although it was clearly not the case, she felt that her sons and daughters were abandoning her. 'I will die there,' Nana proclaimed to her children. 'We all have to die somewhere,' Aunty Florrie retorted. But Aunty Florrie also pointed out to her mother that she would be well looked after at Montefiore.

Nana needn't have worried about a lack of visitors: her children had no intention of leaving her at Montefiore and forgetting about her. Anyway, Nana ultimately had no choice, despite her reservations and protests. She could no longer live alone and she moved into the Montefiore in February 2002.

Grandma Hilda

Ten years younger than Nana and eight years younger than Grandpa, Grandma Hilda was undoubtedly the most youthful of all my grandparents, both in body and mind. Of the three of them, I was unquestionably closest to Grandma.

At the time of my weekly visits to Nana's O'Brien Street apartment to speak to her about our family's history, I also used to visit Grandma and Grandpa in their apartment next door. By that time, Grandpa was unable to recollect much of his early life. But Grandma was always thrilled to have me visit and insisted that I eat something with her. A few times we went out for lunch together – something which Nana and Grandpa were then unable to do – and she was always happy to be out (she loved to be out!) and to be with me. This is how I best like to remember Grandma: smiling, with a zest for life and clad in long sleeves and pants, even on the warmest of Sydney days.

Grandma Hilda was the last of my grandparents to move into the Montefiore Home. To me, Grandma's move to Montefiore was the saddest, but not just because I was closest to her. Unlike Grandpa whose mind started failing him and Nana whose body started failing her, Grandma instead lost her will to live. It is ironic that Grandma, a woman who was so good at nurturing others and so resilient when she had to look after Grandpa for so many years, didn't value her life when she had only herself to care for.

33. GRANDMA'S DECLINE

In early 1999, Grandma travelled to Los Angeles to visit her children and two grandchildren. The trip was to provide her with a much-needed break from looking after Grandpa. He was physically unable to travel with her by this time anyway.

In addition, Grandma's first and adored grandchild, Melissa, had been asking to have Grandma visit her in LA for some time. Melissa had been diagnosed with bipolar disorder and was not well. Having grown up with Grandma nearby, she and Grandma were very close and missed each other terribly when Grandma moved to Sydney. Now that she was sick, Melissa desperately wanted to see her beloved Grandma Hilda.

So Grandpa was put into respite care at the Montefiore Home (this was before he was admitted permanently) and Grandma flew to LA alone, intending to return to Sydney four weeks later. But Grandma's visit ended tragically, with Melissa, only twenty-six years old, dying in March 1999. This was absolutely devastating for our family and, of course, for Grandma. My parents flew to LA for Melissa's funeral and Grandma travelled back to Sydney with them. She was in no state to fly alone.

When Grandma returned to Sydney after Melissa's death, she was exceptionally sad and cried often. But Grandma's grief did not overwhelm her to the point where we were concerned about her; it was to be expected that she would grieve for a long time over Melissa.

Despite Melissa's death, Grandma still had a purpose for living – she had Grandpa to look after. And the fact that Nana lived next door was a blessing for her. Grandma hated to be alone and Nana, although ten years her senior, was a companion for her. When Grandpa had his afternoon rest, Grandma went next door to visit Nana. My two grandmothers drank tea together and chatted – in a way I imagine their own mothers did in Bombay in their old age – and Grandma shared the company of Nana's many children and their families when they stopped by to visit.

By this time, Nana was not very mobile. Grandma was always willing to help – she often declared (in Hindi and English!) that we were put on this earth to do good. So Grandma did bits of shopping for Nana at the nearby supermarket and greengrocer, made her tea and even bathed her from time to time.

I realise now that Grandma thrived on being needed by others. But at the time, it took me by surprise that almost as soon as Grandpa moved to Montefiore, Grandma's health deteriorated rapidly. It was ironic really; I thought that being without Grandpa and all the responsibility of looking after him (and the reality that they'd never been happily married) would be just the freedom that Grandma had always craved. But I was wrong and in fact the opposite was true.

It was not the premature death of her beautiful granddaughter that destroyed Grandma. Rather, it was Grandpa's move to Montefiore, more than two years after Melissa died, which caused Grandma to lose her will to live. Even though she didn't love him, Grandma needed Grandpa in a way I didn't understand.

When Grandpa permanently moved into the Montefiore, Grandma continued to live in their apartment. At seventy-nine years old, she began to live alone for the first time in her life. At first, she had Nana to keep her company, but this situation was only temporary as Nana moved to Montefiore just seven months after Grandpa.

My mother worked very close to Grandma's apartment and

stopped in most afternoons to visit her on her way home from work. Mum often found Grandma's fridge stocked with food that Mum had cooked for her; food that she was supposed to be eating but which remained untouched. Grandma had stopped eating proper meals and was only eating her beloved cake and biscuits, accompanied by cups of tea.

My mother and her siblings became increasingly concerned about Grandma's behaviour. Aunty Mozelle and Uncle Fred, being so far away, deferred to my parents' judgment and recommendations. After much discussion, they agreed that the best option was for Grandma to vacate her O'Brien Street apartment and move into my parents' home.

Grandma's move was preceded by the time-consuming task of my parents sorting through the entire contents of Grandma and Grandpa's apartment. Much of it was sold or given to charity, although my parents did keep a few things for themselves. I inherited only one item: Grandma and Grandpa's sofa. I'd sat on it countless times in their home, often feeling the sea breeze on me while Grandma recounted to me what she'd seen earlier that day on what she insisted on calling the 'Opera' (Oprah Winfrey) show. Today, my grandparents' sofa is well-used in my home and is a constant reminder of them both.

Grandma's move into my parents' house in March 2003 did not, however, solve any problems. Grandma continued to worsen, only now my mother could see just how much Grandma had deteriorated.

Her condition was so bad that she no longer knew right from left. My mother has always kept a kosher kitchen with separate sinks for meat and dairy. She marked them clearly so that Grandma would not get confused, but Grandma nevertheless kept on putting dishes in the wrong sink. I know how much this would have incensed my mother, as when we were growing up, my brother and I nicknamed her 'Beth', short for *Beth Din* (the Jewish rabbinical court which among other things, licences the *Kashrut* Authority) because she was so meticulous about keeping kosher in her kitchen.

Both my parents were incredibly frustrated with Grandma. They tried to engage her in a variety of activities – reading the newspaper, preparing food, going for walks – but although she helped with simple chores around the house, she was essentially uninterested in everything except watching TV.

Although I was no longer living with my parents, I was in close contact with them and it was difficult for me to watch the strain that Grandma's presence was placing on them. Although I loved Grandma, my first loyalty was to my parents and I felt very protective of them. They were clearly exhausted and stressed, but, motivated by love and devotion (and the very strong value of respecting elders), they continued to care for Grandma.

I had no solution to easing my parents' burden as I couldn't comprehend what had happened to Grandma. I didn't understand how she had fallen apart so completely and so quickly. I felt enormously perplexed that she was so uninterested in her own health and wellbeing. And I was angry that she made almost no effort to help around the house and engage in the world around her. What I failed to understand was the power of the connection between Grandma's mind and her body. Although I didn't realise it, by this time Grandma was not consciously choosing to neglect herself. She was now physically incapable of doing otherwise.

My mother obviously had a clearer picture of what was happening with her. At the same time as Grandma moved into my parents' home, my mother put her on the Montefiore waiting list – just in case she needed a place. A place did come up, but it was much earlier than my mother had expected. This created a dilemma: Mum didn't really want Grandma to go to Montefiore so soon, but it was clear that my parents would not be able to care for her on a long-term basis.

My mother spent many sleepless nights trying to make a decision. The idea of sending Grandma to Montefiore made her feel terribly guilty. She didn't want to give up on Grandma, but there was no easy solution. Finally, when Grandma became incontinent, Mum knew she couldn't care for her anymore.

Grandma Hilda was admitted to Montefiore in Hunters Hill in October 2003. She wouldn't last long there.

My memories of the Montefiore Home are fuzzy. It is almost as if I have intentionally blocked them out of my mind since the times that I went there to visit my grandparents were not happy ones.

On my visits to Montefiore, I felt that each of my grandparents were simply treading water, waiting to die. I always left feeling terribly sad that they had become so old and so frail, and so unlike what they had once been.

Consequently, I was not such a regular visitor to the Montefiore Home. Going there was invariably painful; it was especially heartbreaking to see Grandpa in the dementia ward. He no longer recognised me and was a shadow of his former self. I distinctly remember one visit to the Montefiore when I took a close look at the photo of Grandpa on the door to his room. I was actually shocked, as I hardly recognised the unsmiling Eze Jacob of the photo with his head bent and blank expression on his face. This, I realised, was how the Montefiore staff saw Eze Jacob. He barely resembled the Grandpa Eze I knew.

The Montefiore was always busy on Sundays, full of people visiting their loved ones. My parents travelled there every Sunday to visit Grandpa, Nana and, in later years, Grandma. Often, they met up with my father's siblings who were visiting Nana and other members of the Sephardi community who were visiting their parents.

In good weather, my parents took Grandpa into the spacious garden and walked him around and they pushed Nana in her wheelchair. They took Nana, Grandpa and Grandma to the concerts held in the Montefiore auditorium and sang *shbachot* (*Shabbat* melodies) with them. My mother usually took some of her home-baked treats to share with them: chocolate cakes, fruit tarts and Iraqi favourites such as date babas and *kakas*. Often, they went to the on-site cafeteria where they drank tea in winter and ate ice-cream in summer.

The emotional and physical toll on each of my parents was great – the trek to Montefiore was tiring and there was no joy seeing their parents in that condition. It was particularly difficult for my mother.

My father was retired and had the support of his siblings when Nana was at Montefiore. My mother, however, worked virtually full-time for most of the fifteen months that both her parents were at the Montefiore. And during that time, Mum's brother and sister were on the other side of the world in Los Angeles. Mum had sole responsibility for visiting Grandma and Grandpa and ensuring their needs were being met … and taking those middle of the night phone calls from Montefiore when my grandparents were ill.

34. AND THEN THERE WAS ONE

Of my three grandparents, Grandpa Eze lived at Montefiore the longest, for a total of two and a half years. As the weeks and months passed, Grandpa began to speak less and less and eventually became quite subdued. I imagine it is because of Grandpa's quietness that the Montefiore staff commented that he was very easy to please. I certainly would not have used to words 'easy to please' to describe the Eze Jacob I knew.

Grandpa never complained about his new home, although perhaps that was symptomatic of his condition rather than an indication that he was satisfied at Montefiore. 'How are things, Dad?' my mother used to ask him. 'Super dooper,' he'd respond enthusiastically in his all-American lingo.

Despite his memory loss, Grandpa's physical health was good. At eighty-eight years old, he didn't take any medication. He had, however, suffered from respiratory problems for much of his life. It was his body's weakness.

In January 2003 Grandpa was struck with pneumonia. He was so ill that my mother was certain he wouldn't survive. To everyone's surprise, however, Grandpa recovered. It took him a month, but in February 2003 he was discharged from hospital and returned to the Montefiore.

After his bout with pneumonia, Grandpa became very frail and needed to use a walker. By this time his memory was very poor and he barely spoke. When Aunty Mozelle, her husband Martin and Uncle Fred visited from LA in August 2002, Grandpa did not recognise any of them.

Yet in late November 2003, the Director of Nursing at Montefiore remarked that Grandpa actually knew much more of what was going on than we were giving him credit for. It is impossible to know what Grandpa's state of awareness really was. But even if the Director of Nursing was right, it was heartbreaking to see Grandpa so unlike the man he had always been.

In January 2004 Mum received a call from Montefiore to say that Grandpa was very ill and was being taken to Ryde Hospital. He had fluid around his lungs and was struggling to breathe. My mother thought Grandpa's illness would be a repeat of his pneumonia a year earlier and that he would pull through. But it wasn't the same this time.

On 23 January 2004, the same day he was taken to hospital, Grandpa suffered a heart attack and died. He was eighty-nine years old. The timing of Grandpa's death took my mother completely by surprise and the chain of events so sudden that Grandpa was all alone when he passed away.

Unbelievably, Aunty Mozelle was in Sydney at the time Grandpa died. She had actually flown out specifically to see Grandma after Grandma had major surgery. Aunty Mozelle had used frequent flyer points to book her flights home and she was unable to book the dates she originally wanted. Had she received her first choice of flights, she would not have been in Sydney to see her father just before his death.

Grandpa Eze was buried in Sydney on 27 January 2004. Uncle Fred arrived from LA the day before the funeral (although Jewish law dictates that burial is to occur as soon as possible after death, there was a delay in releasing Grandpa's body which allowed Uncle Fred to be in Sydney for the funeral despite the long flight from LA). It was enormously comforting for my mother to have Aunty Mozelle and Uncle Fred by her side at the funeral.

This was particularly so given that Grandma didn't attend Grandpa's funeral. In fact, Grandma wasn't even told of her husband's death, because she was in no condition to sit *shiva* (the week-long period of grief and mourning prescribed by Jewish law).

At the time Grandpa died, Grandma was living at the Montefiore Home, but their rooms were in completely different sections of the Home and they had little to do with each other. The Montefiore staff and my parents' rabbi agreed it was best that Grandma not be told of Grandpa's death because they were concerned it would cause Grandma, who had just had hip replacement surgery and wasn't recovering well, to deteriorate even further.

While my mother and her two siblings sat *shiva* at my parents' home, the Benjamin family and members of the Sephardi community prayed, visited and brought seemingly endless amounts of food for seven days. The support that our family received that week was wonderful. Interestingly, during this week when my parents' home was filled with people each evening, Uncle Fred commented that there was much more of a sense of community in Sydney than there was in Los Angeles. This is exactly what my mother had felt when she'd lived in LA some thirty years earlier.

Still, the *shiva* week was not an easy one. My mother was torn between grieving for her father and caring for her sick mother. Technically, mourners are required to remain at the home in which they are sitting *shiva* for the entire seven days. However, my mother and her siblings visited Grandma at the Montefiore every day during the *shiva* period, except on *Shabbat*, as Aunty Mozelle and Uncle Fred didn't know when they'd see Grandma again. It was a physically and emotionally exhausting week.

For me, Grandpa's death was undoubtedly sad, but it also brought a sense of relief: relief that he was no longer suffering and relief that my mother would not have to be in a constant state of worry about his health. At the same time, Grandpa's passing suddenly pushed the issues of death and mortality to the forefront of my mind.

I was incredibly fortunate to have been twenty-eight years old before I had to face the death of any of my grandparents (excluding Papa Jacob as he'd died before I was born). After Grandpa died, I was left with only one living grandparent – Grandma Hilda.

My other grandmother, Nana Hannah, had died only three months before Grandpa Eze.

35. FINAL GOODBYES

Whereas Grandpa settled in relatively well at Montefiore, Nana – who had resisted moving there anyway – was not happy in her new home. She complained bitterly about how much she disliked the Montefiore, especially the mass-produced food. In her last few months there, all Nana's food had to be pureed because she couldn't swallow. She had always taken so much pride in cooking tasty meals, and she detested the bland and untextured puree.

Eventually though, Nana did accept her place at Montefiore. Her fears that she would be alone there without visitors proved completely unfounded. With most of her children and grandchildren living in Sydney, Nana received visitors regularly.

Determined to the end, Nana lasted two years at Montefiore. Even though she didn't like being there, she never gave up her will to live.

It is amazing how the last few weeks of her life seem clearer to me than so many of my other memories of her. The days, weeks and months of growing up in her presence have melded into one large, all-encompassing memory. In contrast, the last time I saw Nana conscious is a distinct memory all of its own.

On Friday 10 October 2003 I went with my parents to the Montefiore. When we arrived, my parents went to visit Grandpa Eze and I went straight to see Nana. I arrived in her room to find her lying in her bed, apparently sleeping. However, she was not at all peaceful and every thirty seconds or so she cried out the word 'ayee'. I didn't know what it meant and I wasn't even sure Nana was asleep, but it was obvious to me that she was in a substantial amount of pain. I later found out that *ayee* is Hindi for 'ouch'.

Nana's nurse told me that Nana was being given morphine to manage her pain. Soon after, Nana awoke and the nurse dressed her in a yellow dress that I recognised from long ago. Once dressed and sitting up in her wheelchair, I noticed that Nana's face was swollen. Her feet and hands were swollen too, as a result of the morphine.

My parents arrived in Nana's room after visiting Grandpa. 'When y'awl (you all) got here?' she enquired of them, in her typical Indian-English constructed sentence. As always, Nana wanted to know exactly what was happening.

We pushed Nana in her wheelchair to the Montefiore café where I fed her some vanilla ice-cream. The irony of the situation did not escape me: Hannah Benjamin, who had raised nine children and prepared thousands of meals for them, could not even feed herself anymore.

Yet I still left Montefiore that day not realising how serious Nana's condition really was.

That same night, Nana was transferred from the Montefiore Home to Sydney's Royal North Shore Hospital. The doctors decided that Nana's left leg had to be amputated due to an infection caused by an ulcer on her foot. Nana had had the ulcer for years but it never healed properly due to the diabetes she had developed towards the end of her life.

The operation was scheduled for the following Tuesday, 14 October 2003. Nana knew exactly what was happening to her; the morning of her operation, my father, Aunty Florrie and Uncle Sammy went to visit her. She announced, 'You know they're going to amputate my foot.' Of course they knew.

Aunty Florrie recalls that Nana was very brave in the face of this development. Aunty Florrie, Uncle Sammy and my father walked Nana right to the operating theatre and were there when she awoke from the anaesthetic. The operation was successful, with no complications. Nana was completely lucid after the operation and, as always, knew all the comings and goings of her visitors. The day after her operation, she remarked to my cousin Ruth, 'Your mother [my aunty Margaret] hasn't come to see me.'

Nana's medical team planned to send Nana back to Montefiore in a few days. But two days after the operation, something in Nana's chest sounded unusual. My father recalls that neither he nor his siblings were concerned about this as they thought it was only a minor issue. But on the Thursday night, Nana was transferred to cardiac care. At 10.00 p.m. that night, Nana turned to Aunty Florrie and asked her, 'What's the time?' Those were Nana's last words ever.

Soon after, Nana took a bad turn and never regained consciousness. The very last time I saw my grandmother, she was lying in a hospital bed with an oxygen mask strapped to her face. She was unconscious but I talked to her and told her that I loved her. I knew she could hear me.

It was clear that Nana would not survive for much longer. On Sunday night 19 October 2003, on the Jewish festival of Simchat Torah, the Hospital called to tell Nana's children to come and say their goodbyes. My father Abe, my brother and Aunty Florrie arrived first and they started reading *tehillim* (psalms). The rest of Nana's children (except Elaine in Israel) arrived soon after.

In the last few hours of Nana's life, her children spoke to her and reassured her they were with her. 'Mummy, you're going to a better place,' Aunty Florrie told her. 'You're going to Daddy.' Each of Nana's children put Nana's hands on their heads and instructed her to bless them and to bless their children.

Aunty Florrie has described Nana's last few hours as being 'like the sun setting'. Nana, who always seemed so fearless to me, was terrified of dying. But her passing was very peaceful and Nana died with eight of her nine children by her side, together with three of her grandchildren.

Hannah Benjamin died in the early hours of 20 October 2003 at Royal North Shore Hospital. She had never wanted to die at Montefiore anyway. She was ninety-one years old and survived her husband Jacob by exactly forty-seven years and two days.

When Nana died, I was asleep in a country town on the New South Wales coast, some seven hours drive from Sydney. My husband and I drove back to Sydney for Nana's funeral, and in the week that we had intended to spend on holiday, we instead spent time with my father and his brothers and sisters as they sat *shiva* for their mother.

Nana's children sat *shiva* at Aunty Mabel's house, just down the road from where I lived. I was there every day and I had a lot of time to think in that week, particularly about what Nana had achieved in her ninety-one years. Nana's death made it abundantly clear to me that what is important in life is not what we have, but who we are and what we will be remembered for. In Nana's case, at the time of her death, she had fifty-eight direct descendants living in Australia, Israel and London. They are her legacy.

On the Friday night during the week of *shiva*, every one of Nana's children, grandchildren and great grandchildren who were in Sydney at the time gathered together. For the first time ever, we ate *Shabbat* dinner together (there were simply too many of us to do this under normal circumstances). In true Benjamin style, there was more food than we possibly could have eaten – except for the strictly rationed beetroot *coobas*, which many of us hadn't eaten since the last time Nana cooked them for us. And in typical Benjamin fashion, my aunts and uncles took the opportunity to urge my cousins and me to get married if we were not already married; to have children if we didn't yet have any; and if we already had children, well then, to have some more.

Grandma Hilda joined us that night for *Shabbat* dinner.

In times gone by, she would have joined the banter and singing which accompanied our meal. The Benjamins, of course, were no strangers to her; many of them affectionately addressed her by a name she'd often been called in India: 'Haboo', short for her Hebrew name, Habiba. Grandma was considered part of my father's family. But sadly, she only sat at the table silently, with hardly even a smile on her face.

One of my grandmothers was no longer alive. But my other grandmother, who was still living, seemed to be wishing her precious life away. Her zest for life had vanished.

36. GRANDMA'S LAST MONTHS

Although Grandma had been in respite care at Montefiore a few times, in October 2003 she moved to the Montefiore Home permanently. I went to visit her at my parents' home only hours before she left for Montefiore. She was wearing my mother's blue dressing gown and was sobbing. Grandma was never in favour of leaving my parents' home for Montefiore and when Mum told her of the decision, Grandma retorted, 'Why are you getting rid of me so quickly?' Grandma's words echoed in my mother's ears for many months afterwards.

And during those months, my mother second-guessed her decision to send Grandma to Montefiore. It caused Mum so much angst that she could hardly sleep at night. And Grandma didn't make it any easier by stubbornly refusing to speak to my mother as revenge when Mum went to visit.

Montefiore's Director of Nursing reassured Mum that Grandma was okay and that she was interacting with the Montefiore staff. Mum later discovered that Grandma was speaking to some of the Indian Montefiore staff in Hindustani, which they were very surprised to hear from a very un-Indian looking Jewish woman. It was then Mum realised that Grandma was intentionally being silent with her. Grandma was furious at my mother for sending her to the Montefiore Home.

Two months after Grandma moved into Montefiore, Mum brought her home for a weekend break. She didn't smile the entire time.

At one point during the weekend, Mum asked Grandma if she preferred to be at the Montefiore or outdoors. She replied that she preferred Montefiore. This was the ultimate indicator that Grandma was no longer the Hilda Jacob we once knew. The Hilda we knew always hated to be inside and would spend all day outdoors if she could. The woman inhabiting her body was a stranger.

In early January 2004, Mum got a call from Montefiore to say that Grandma had fallen over and was being taken to hospital via ambulance. Six days later, Grandma underwent hip replacement surgery.

Grandma's post-operative recovery was not good. She didn't want to eat or drink, refused to take her medication and wouldn't let the nurses touch her. Her physiotherapy progressed slowly and she barely ate, which meant her body was very slow to heal. Although Grandma loved to walk, she never walked after her surgery and was confined to a wheelchair. It was extremely sad and frustrating for us to watch Grandma in this state, particularly because she seemed so completely uninterested in her recovery.

By early February, Grandma had made some form of recovery from the surgery and was back at Montefiore. But she still didn't make any conversation and wasn't eating properly. Only a few weeks later, Grandma was again taken to hospital, this time suffering from dehydration. While she was there she had to be given two iron infusions because she'd become so anaemic. When Grandma was transferred back to the Montefiore ten days later and my parents went to visit, they managed to feed her a bit and Grandma actually talked to them, much to my mother's delight.

But that visit was an exception. Grandma generally spoke so little that when she commented to Mum after a Montefiore concert that 'the music is so beautiful,' Mum was actually shocked.

The last time I saw Grandma she was only a shadow of her former self. It was the day of her eighty-second birthday in May

2004 and I went with my parents, brother and husband to visit her. In her usual organised fashion, my mother brought a cake and organised drinks. Grandma sat in a wheelchair in the gardens of the Montefiore Home with a shawl around her to keep her warm. She looked pale and weak, didn't smile and spoke only to my brother. Even then, it was only a few words. It was awful to see her like that.

At the time, I was three months pregnant with my first child. Mum was so excited for me to tell Grandma the news, hoping it would lift her spirits. But I was dreading it because I knew Grandma wouldn't share the excitement.

When I told her I was pregnant, Grandma nodded in acknowledgement. But as I predicted, she failed to comprehend the implications of my news. Even though I'd expected that reaction, I was somehow disappointed. Not so long ago, Grandma would have been overjoyed to find out she was to become a great-grandmother. Now, she didn't even seem to care.

Grandma only survived a few months after her eighty-second birthday. And it really was surviving rather than living; her quality of life was exceptionally poor.

At the end of June 2004, my mother quit her job to spend time with Grandma, knowing there wouldn't be much time left. Aunty Mozelle, her family and Uncle Fred had booked flights to Sydney for August 2004 for Grandpa's consecration and to visit Grandma. But even Mum didn't expect that after leaving work she would only get three weeks with her mother and that Grandma wouldn't make it to see her LA-based family.

Aunty Mozelle's suitcases, including two boxes of Grandma's favourite cinnamon Cheerios, were already packed when Grandma died. It was *Tisha B'Av* (the ninth day of the Hebrew month of Av), 26 July 2004. Fittingly, a day of mourning for the Jewish people (both the Temples were destroyed on *Tisha B'Av* and many other catastrophes occurred to the Jewish people on this day) and for our family.

Despite the joy of the impending birth of my first child, it was a terribly sad time for me. I remember walking down Sydney's busy city streets on my way to work and being unable to stop crying while streams of people walked past me. I was glad that Grandma was out of her pain, as I knew she had lost the will to live. But I was so sad that she hadn't understood that her first great-grandchild was soon to be born. Or that if by some chance I was wrong and she had understood, that she hadn't found it worth living for. The Grandma of a few years earlier would have been excited beyond belief.

Mum and Dad never told Grandma directly that Grandpa had passed away. Yet my mother is almost certain that by the time Grandma died, she knew Grandpa was no longer alive. In the week after his death, my parents found a letter in her drawer sent by the Montefiore which offered condolences on the passing of her dear husband. But Grandma never mentioned that she'd received the letter, nor did she demonstrate any awareness of its contents. Only once did Grandma talk about Grandpa after he died, and even then, it was only a brief comment: about a month after he passed away, Grandma told my mother to talk to Grandpa and to watch out for him.

It is puzzling that Grandma never asked after Grandpa. But if my mother is right and Grandma did know that Grandpa had died, I don't understand why she didn't discuss it. Then again, there are so many things I don't understand about Grandma's last year of life that it's impossible for me to gauge what Grandma really knew about Grandpa's death

I was blessed to have the only three grandparents I had ever known alive at my wedding in Sydney in December 2000. Less than four

years later, and within less than a year of each other, not one of them was alive.

Only months after Grandma Hilda died, my first child – a daughter, Zara (meaning 'princess', 'dawn'; a variation on the name of Sara, one of the four biblical matriarchs) was born. And just short of four years later, my second child – a son, Asher (meaning 'blessed', 'happiness') was born.

And now it is my own parents who are grandparents. My mother and father live less than a ten-minute walk away from us and play a significant role in my children's lives. *Savta* (Hebrew for 'grandmother') Sheila and *Saba* (Hebrew for 'grandfather') Abe are Zara and Asher's adored grandparents and are involved in their childhoods in a way that my grandparents were never involved in mine. It is one of my greatest joys to see my mother and father's faces light up when they see my children.

That joy is magnified knowing that my mother didn't have the day to day support of her parents while she was raising my brother and me (as they were living in LA) and that my father did not have his father to guide him for all of his adult life.

In my role as a mother, I am awed at my grandmothers and my mother, who raised their children under much harsher conditions than I am doing. Now that I am a mother, I can't fathom how Mum made it through her early years in Australia with two small children and no family of her own. And as a parent, I understand how my grandfather Jacob's death impacted on my father's life, in a way I could not appreciate before I had my own children.

I've also gained glimpses of how it feels for my parents to be without their parents – my grandparents. At the same time as my mother and father delight in playing with Zara and Asher, the losses of Grandma Hilda, Grandpa Eze, Nana Hannah and Papa Jacob are ever-present. Not just for Mum and Dad, but for me too.

37. THE NEXT GENERATION

Much has changed over the course of three generations in my family. My children, unlike me, my parents and grandparents, are not fully Sephardi. As their father is an Ashkenazi Jew, Zara and Asher are 'Ashkephardi': part Sephardi, part Ashkenazi. And while I am first generation Australian, my children are second generation Australian. These differences mean that the way they are growing up in Sydney is significantly different from the way I did.

I am the child of immigrants. So although I was born in Australia, I have always felt an affinity with India. And although I am a Sephardi Jew, I grew up in an Ashkenazi-dominated Jewish community. These conflicting forces: Sephardi versus Ashkenazi, Australia versus India pulled me in different directions and were always difficult for me to reconcile. Particularly the Sephardi/Ashkenazi one.

All my formal education took place in Jewish day schools. I attended a Jewish kindergarten and then went to Jewish primary and high schools. Yet throughout my schooling I was one of only a handful of Sephardi Jews in a sea of Ashkenazim. Most of the Sephardi children in my primary school were my cousins and by the time I reached high school, the Sephardi Jewish presence was completely subsumed by the Ashkenazi majority. The school curriculum did not encompass the history of Iraqi-Sephardi Jewry, the prayer tunes sung were Ashkenazi and the Jewish laws and customs taught were those of Ashkenazi Jewry.

As I grew up, I learnt very quickly that none of my friends ate apple jam on *Rosh Hashana* (Jewish New Year), that what my mother called *kotmir* everyone else called coriander, and that not all children eagerly awaited the arrival of *shasha* (lolly bags) to herald the birth of a new baby into the family. In fact, most of the practices my family followed were completely foreign even to my Jewish friends and their families, although they were jealously aware that I was able to eat rice on *Pesach* (Passover).

I don't think my parents even realised the inconsistency or how torn I felt. They sent me to a Jewish school which they presumed would provide me with a Jewish education and reinforce the Jewish values and traditions I was being brought up with at home. But the Jewish education I received did not echo a lot of what was going on in my home.

As such, I always felt that I was straddling two worlds: the world of the Benjamin family, with its inextricable connection to Bombay, and the world of Sydney's Jewish community, of which I am undoubtedly a part but which is predominantly Ashkenazi. Even today, I feel as if I have one foot in each camp and that I don't quite belong in either. I sometimes wonder whether this feeling of being an outsider will ever completely disappear.

Interestingly, over twenty years ago Naomi Gale, a Sydney Sephardi Jew, noted in her PhD thesis that (Australian) Jewish day schools do little to evoke Sephardi pride (the only Jewish identity is Ashkenazi).[46] She concluded that the 'continual process of acculturation … will probably result in its [the Australian Sephardi community's] disappearance as a viable "community" within a generation.'[47]

This dire forecast has not yet come true. However, I consider that unless there is a dramatic change to the status quo, it is only a matter of time before Naomi's prediction is realised.

Like me, my children will not be educated about their Sephardi heritage in any formal learning environment. There is no program – either in the Jewish day school system or outside it – which teaches Jewish children the history and customs of the Baghdadi Jews. This leaves individual family units and Sydney's Sephardi Synagogue as the primary, if not only, institutions which can pass down the religious observances of the Baghdadi Jews to the next generations.

In terms of the family unit, my Sephardi contemporaries, almost without exception, have married Ashkenazi Jews. Their children, like mine, are receiving a watered-down version of the Sephardi traditions with which we were brought up. Even though *halacha* (Jewish law) dictates that when a woman marries, she is to take on the customs of her husband (and therefore a Sephardi bride is to take on the customs of her Ashkenazi groom), I expect that it is only in particularly religious households that this occurs. In my family, for example, we incorporate both Sephardi and Ashkenazi prayer tunes, observances and customs into our daily life.

Nevertheless, my children are not exposed to the same range of Baghdadi Jewish practices that I was while I was growing up. And their children will therefore have even less exposure as the Baghdadi Jewish influence is further diluted.

As for Sydney's Sephardi Synagogue, it is true to say that the Ashkenazi spouses of many of my Sephardi contemporaries are affiliated with the Synagogue. But the Sephardi Synagogue has not, at least to my knowledge, recognised that without major involvement on its part, the Baghdadi traditions on which it is based will eventually die out.

The Synagogue is still very full on all the major *chagim* (festivals) and there is apparently a waiting list to become a member of the congregation. However, the core community – the men and women who regularly attend services and are on the Board of Management – is an ageing one. On an ordinary *Shabbat* morning service, there are only a handful of women and even fewer children who attend regularly. And most of the men who attend have grown children, even grandchildren. In contrast, when I was a child, the Synagogue was full of young families and children – families who were committed to the future of the Synagogue.

Only now, the future of the Synagogue seems uncertain. Who will be its future leaders? And what will be the composition of the community in twenty, thirty, forty years time? The Synagogue's membership today is already significantly different from the Synagogue my father became a member of some fifty years ago. Whereas in the past, most members were Sephardi, today there are many Ashkenazi members. Eventually, it may be that the Baghdadi mode of prayer will become obsolete as the Sephardi membership dies out without being replaced.

To me, the future of Sydney's Sephardi community looks bleak. Of the two worlds between which I have always been torn – Sephardi and Ashkenazi – I expect that my children will fall more squarely into the Ashkenazi one. And that their children will observe few, if any, Baghdadi Jewish customs.

Sadly, I believe that in the not so distant future, the richness of my heritage will be relegated to a mere chapter in the long history of the Jewish people.

EPILOGUE

My kitchen doesn't contain a dedicated spice cupboard like my mother had while I was growing up. But my pantry doors are lined with spice racks containing all the spices I need to prepare the Indian and Iraqi food I grew up eating. And it is my daughter who can name all my spices and who loves to smell their different aromas.

Zara has been baking *chapatis* with Savta Sheila since before she could even say the word '*chapati*'. Just like me, Zara loves to eat my mother's delicious *chapatis* and from the age of one and a half would demand '*pati mor*' – more *chapatis* – from her grandmother. Asher's latest development is to ask for a 'special treat' at virtually all meal and snack times. He is particularly fond of Savta Sheila's *kakas*, which she prepares especially for her egg- and dairy-intolerant grandson in quantities that would be sufficient to feed our entire family for at least a month.

In our backyard, we are growing a small curry leaf plant. It started as a cutting taken from my parents' huge curry leaf tree and it is flourishing. I use the curry leaves on the rare occasions that I have time to prepare dishes like *aloo bhaji* and fish curry. In the meantime, Zara likes to pull the small leaves off the plant and show them to guests who have never even heard of a curry leaf plant. The visitors are surprised to discover that the leaves really do smell like curry.

We occasionally go out with my parents for meals at Indian restaurants. Their favourite is a casual Indian vegetarian restaurant named Maya, where they also sometimes go with my aunts and uncles. Whenever any of the Benjamins go to Maya or any other Indian restaurant, they chat to the Indian wait staff and are sure to mention that they are from Bombay. The restaurant staff are invariably delighted, although usually a little surprised, to have these men and women who don't look at all Indian able to converse in Hindustani and so familiar with the menu items.

My mother has taught Zara a few words of Hindustani. 'Don't be a *sooky bhaji*', Zara chastises her brother when he is whingeing. Asher, in fact, is a bit cheeky and is known as *musty wallah* (mischievous person). Zara understands that when I say *buss* while someone pours me a drink, it means I have enough. And when I get cranky, Zara has been known to ask rhetorically, 'Your *hasoofad*, right?' knowing my *hasoofad* – whatever that may be – has gone. That I have lost my patience.

On Friday nights in our home, I lead the singing of the *Shabbat* hymn *Eshet Chayil* ('A Woman of Valour'). I sing the same tune that I grew up hearing – the Baghdadi one. Zara, now six, has memorised most of the words and can sing along with me. She doesn't yet realise that our *erev Shabbat* (Friday night) prayers are a mixture of Sephardi and Ashkenazi tunes and *brachot* (blessings).

As for the Sephardi Synagogue, it continues to be a very important part of my parents' lives. They attend services almost every *Shabbat* and my father is a regular reader from the Torah. Almost all of the extended Benjamin family who live in Sydney affiliate with the Synagogue.

I have mixed feelings about the Synagogue. Even though the building was completely renovated some ten years ago, going to Sephardi Synagogue takes me back to my childhood, a place where I feel completely protected and safe. To me, going there still feels like going home. I love sitting upstairs in the women's section next to my mother with my children by our sides, with my Aunty Florrie close by and my father, my husband and my brother downstairs. I love seeing the familiar faces of people I have known all my life.

But as much as the Sephardi Synagogue is part of me, I love it for the place it occupies in my heart rather than what it has to offer me and my family today. Due to the absence of young families on a regular *Shabbat* morning, we rarely attend services there. We do, however, pray there occasionally, such as during the *chagim* (festivals) when I feel drawn to being there with my extended family, or if there is a Benjamin *simcha* like a bar mitzvah.

I have come to realise that although I completely identify as a Sephardi Jew, my religious observance is a mix of Sephardi and Ashkenazi practices. For me, being a Sephardi Jew is less about adhering to strict religious practices and more about a way of life. Certainly, that life is underpinned by Judaism: the weekly celebration of *Shabbat*, the observance of the *chagim* and the sharing of life cycle events with family, friends and community. But it is more than that. It is a life influenced by the Iraqi and Indian origins of my parents and grandparents, and a life filled with warmth, love, hospitality and, of course, delicious food.

To me, the essence of being a Baghdadi Jew can be captured in one Arabic colloquial word: *awafi*. The literal meaning of *awafi* is 'to your health', but this translation does not capture the spirit of this word. Before starting a meal, diners in some cultures wish each other *bon appetit* or in Hebrew, *betayavon*. In contrast, the Iraqi Jews wait until after the meal when the host or hostess can see that their guests have enjoyed the food and eaten all they can. Only then will they will proudly announce the word '*awafi*'.[48]

Although I never say *awafi* after serving a meal, it is certainly one of my great pleasures to prepare food which my husband and children enjoy eating. Even better are the meals which my mother cooks for us (often hand delivered to the front door of our home by my father). Mum's food is prepared with so much love that it nourishes not only my body, but also my soul. When I call her to thank her for the food and report back how delicious it was, she invariably replies: '*awafi*'. The utterance of that one word manages to convey so many things. Perhaps most importantly, it ensures that I can never forget the journey of the previous generations of my family from Baghdad to Bombay to Bondi.

Bondi, 2011
Back row (left to right): Mike, Asher, Elana
Front row: Sheila, Zara, Abe

ENDNOTES

1   Gubbay, L. & Levy, A., *The Sephardim: Their Glorious Tradition From the Babylonian Exile to the Present Day*, Carnell, London, 1992, at 71

2   http://www.moia.gov.il/Moia_en/AboutIsrael/ezraVenechmia.htm

3   Benjamin, M., *Last Days in Babylon: The Story of the Jews of Baghdad*, Bloomsbury, Great Britain, 2007, at 142

4   ibid., at 174

5   www.moia.gov.il, op. cit.

6   Benjamin, op. cit., at 178

7   http://www.jewishvirtuallibrary.org/jsource/anti-semitism/iraqijews.html

8   Roland, J. G., *Jews in British India: Identity in a Colonial Era¸* University Press of New England, Hanover, 1989, at 15

9   Jackson, S., *The Sassoons*, Heinemann, London, 1968, at 5

10 ibid., at 39

11 Roland, op. cit., at 17

12 Roland, op. cit., at 18

13 Roland, op. cit., at 136

14 Slapak, O. (ed.), *The Jews of India: A Story of Three Communities*, The Israel Museum, Jerusalem, 1995, at 9

15 ibid., at 43

16 Roland, op. cit., at 144

17 ibid.

18 ibid.

19   ibid.

20   ibid.

21   ibid., at 133

22   ibid., at 133–4

23   ibid., at 254

24   Isenberg, S. B., 'The Jews of India: Collating the Data and Suggestions for Further Research', in Timberg, T. A. (ed.), *Jews in India*, Advent Books, New York, 1986, at 57

25   Katz, N., *Who Are the Jews of India?*, University of California Press, Berkeley, 2000, at 145

26   ibid., at 143–5

27   Jackson, op. cit., at 3

28   Abram, D. et al., *India The Rough Guide* (3rd edition), Rough Guides Ltd, London, 1999, at 686

29   ibid., at 677

30   ibid.

31   ibid.

32   ibid., at 682

33   Roland, op. cit., at 242

34   ibid., 248

35   ibid., at 251

36   ibid., at 263

37   Slapak, op. cit., at 43

38   Roland, op. cit., at 241

39   ibid., at 248

40   ibid., at 251

41   Aaron, A., *The Sephardim of Australia and New Zealand*, Aaron Aaron, Australia, 1979, at 77

42 Stember, C. H. et al, *Jews in the Mind of America*, New York, Basic Books, 1966, at 17

43 Sherman, C. B., *The Jew Within American Society*, Wayne State University Press, Michigan, 1960, at 64

44 Greenwood, H., *Good Living, The Sydney Morning Herald*, 19–25 February 2002, at 5

45 The Montefiore Home was first established in 1888

46 Gale, N., *From the Homeland to Sydney: Kinship, Religion and Ethnicity among Sephardim*, The University of Sydney, 1988, at 402

47 ibid., at 411

48 Gubbay, M., Isaac, M. & Gubbay-Nemes, G. (eds.), *Awafi: Exotic Cuisine from the Middle and Far East*, NSW Association of Sephardim, NSW, 1990, at 7

BIBLIOGRAPHY

Aaron, Aaron, *The Sephardim of Australia and New Zealand*, Aaron Aaron, Australia, 1979

Abram, David, et al., *India The Rough Guide* (3rd edition), Rough Guides Ltd, London, 1999

Benjamin, Marina, *Last Days in Babylon: The Story of the Jews of Baghdad*, Bloomsbury, Great Britain, 2007

Bhende, Asha A. & Jhirad, Ralphy E., *Demographic and Socio-Economic Characterstics of Jews in India*, ORT India, Mumbai,1997

De Lange, Nicholas, *The Illustrated History of the Jewish People*, Aurum Press, Great Britain, 1997

Gale, N., *From the Homeland to Sydney: Kinship, Religion and Ethnicity among Sephardim*, The University of Sydney, 1988

Greenwood, H., *Good Living, The Sydney Morning Herald*, 19–25 February 2002

Gubbay, Lucien & Levy, Abraham, *The Sephardim: Their Glorious Tradition From the Babylonian Exile to the Present Day*, Carnell, London, 1992

Gubbay, M., Isaac, M. & Gubbay-Nemes, G. (eds), *Awafi: Exotic Cuisine from the Middle and Far East*, NSW Association of Sephardim, NSW, 1990

Hyman, Mavis, *Indian-Jewish Cooking*, Hyman Publishers, London, 1992.

Hyman, Mavis, *Jews of the Raj*, Hyman Publishers, London, 1995

Israel, Benjamin J., *The Jews of India*, Mosaic Books, New Delhi, 1998

Jackson, Stanley, *The Sassoons*, Heinemann, London, 1968

Katz, Nathan, *Studies of Indian Jewish Identity*, Manohar, New Delhi, 1995

Katz, Nathan, *Who Are the Jews of India?*, University of California Press, Berkeley, 2000

Morad, Tamar, Shasha, Dennis and Shasha, Robert (eds.), *Iraq's Last Jews: Stories of Daily Life, Upheaval, and Escape from Modern Babylon*, Palgrave Macmillan, United States, 2008

Roden, Claudia, *The Book of Jewish Food: An Odyssey from Samarkand and Vilna to the Present Day*, Viking, Great Britain, 1997

Roland, Joan G., *Jews in British India: Identity in a Colonial Era*, University Press of New England, Hanover, 1989

Sherman, Charles B., *The Jew Within American Society*, Wayne State University Press, Michigan, 1960

Slapak, Orpa (ed.), *The Jews of India: A Story of Three Communities*, The Israel Museum, Jerusalem, 1995

Stember, Charles H. et al., *Jews in the Mind of America*, New York, Basic Books, 1966

Timberg, Thomas A. (ed.), *Jews in India*, Advent Books, New York, 1986

Weil, Shalva (ed.), *India's Jewish Heritage: Ritual, Art & Life-Cycle*, Marg Publications, Mumbai, 2002

FROM MY BOOKSHELF

A list of notable memoirs which influenced and inspired me while writing *My Mother's Spice Cupboard*

Jewish

Armstrong, Diane, *Mosaic: A Chronicle of Five Generations*, Random House, Australia, 1998

Behmoiras, Josiane, *My Mother Was A Bag Lady*, Bloomsbury, London, 2007

Delman, Carmit, *Burnt Bread and Chutney: Growing Up Between Cultures – A Memoir of an Indian Jewish Girl*, Ballantine, USA, 2002

Lagnado, Lucette, *The Man in the White Sharkskin Suit: A Jewish Family's Exodus from Old Cairo to the New World*, Ecco/Harper Collins, USA, 2007

Tayar, Aline P'nina, *How Shall We Sing: A Mediterranean Journey Through a Jewish Family*, Pan Macmillan/Picador, Australia, 2000

Food, The Immigrant Experience

Contini, Mary, *Dear Francesca: A Family Memoir of Life, Love and Cooking*, Bantam, Australia, 2002

Do, Anh, *The Happiest Refugee: My Journey from Tragedy to Comedy*, Allen & Unwin, Australia, 2010

Fedler, Joanne, *When Hungry, Eat*, Allen & Unwin, Australia, 2010

Travel

Macdonald, Sarah, *Holy Cow: An Indian Adventure*, Bantam, Australia, 2002

Turnbull, Sarah, *Almost French: A New Life in Paris*, Bantam, Australia, 2002

Resilience

Fox, Michael J, *Lucky Man: A Memoir*, Hyperion, USA, 2002

Fox, Michael J, *Always Looking Up: The Adventures of an Incurable Optomist*, Hyperion, USA, 2009